A Source Book of Classic Cars

A Source Book of
Classic Cars

Written and compiled by G. N. Georgano

WARD LOCK LIMITED · LONDON

Frontispiece picture: 1929 Duesenberg

© Ward Lock Limited 1977

ISBN 0 7063 5039 1

First published in Great Britain in 1977
by Ward Lock Limited, 116 Baker Street,
London, W1M 2BB, a member of the Pentos Group.

Text filmset in Univers

Printed and bound in Great Britain by
Cox & Wyman Ltd,
London, Fakenham and Reading

Acknowledgments

The Author and Publishers would like to thank the following for
their generous help in providing information and photographs:

B. T. Batsford & Co. Ltd
William Boddy
Chrysler Historical Collection
George Dammann
Detroit Public Library
Hugh Durnford
James Edwards (Harrah's Automobile Collection)
Edward Gaylord
Thomas H. Hubbard
George A. Ingram
Frank Kurtis
Bjorn-Eric Lindh
Lucien Loreille
Strother McMinn
Keith Marvin
Bruce Baldwin Mohs
National Motor Museum at Beaulieu
Vaclav Petrik
Sir John Richmond
Rolls-Royce Motors Ltd
Edgar E. Rohr
Michael Sedgwick
Dick Sommerin
Kenneth H. Stauffer
Frank Woollen
Stan Yost

Introduction

The expression 'classic car' has many interpretations. The Classic Car Club of America caters for cars of superior quality built between the years 1925 and 1942, while in Britain the magazine *Classic Car* covers interesting cars of any period, but more particularly the high-performance machines of the post-war era. In this book we are interpreting the word 'classic' in its broadest sense, to include outstanding cars of every era, but especially those of high quality aimed at a small group of discriminating buyers.

The book starts with the 60 hp Mercedes of 1903, for this was the first car in which long-distance touring could be undertaken with reasonable speed and comfort, surely two essential elements of classic motoring. During the years up to the outbreak of war in 1914 the quality car developed rapidly, so that the best cars of 1914 could stand comparison with many that were being made in the 1920s. Many people think that Rolls-Royce never made a car so completely satisfying to drive as the four-speed Silver Ghost of 1914. These were the years when the six-cylinder engine became universal for large cars; the four was considered too rough, though a few four-cylinder monsters such as the 90 hp Mercedes and the Type KM Isotta-Fraschini lingered on, while the V-8 was barely established.

The inter-war years saw the finest flowering of the luxury car, and the choice of vehicles that can be considered as classics was enormous. Although the war had impoverished some people, it had enriched many others: the 'war profiteers' so often ridiculed in cartoons and sketches. In America the motion-picture industry was producing considerable numbers of newly rich stars and producers. All these people were customers for expensive cars, and manufacturers were not slow to meet the demand. In addition to established firms like Rolls-Royce and Packard, new companies sprang up everywhere. In France the aircraft industry was a springboard for several manufacturers such as Voisin, Farman, and Gnome-Rhône. The aviator Réné Fonck turned his hand to car making, as did his American equivalent Eddie Rickenbacker. In England lorry makers such as Leyland, Guy and British Ensign entered the quality-car field, though none of these survived for very long.

The 1920s saw the zenith of the custom body, for the majority of luxury cars were supplied in chassis form only. In most cases the customer was happy to leave the radiator and bonnet unchanged, for to ride behind the wheel of Rolls-Royce's Silver Lady or Hispano-Suiza's *Cigogne Volante* conferred great prestige, regardless of the bodywork. However, in America there was a vogue for totally disguising the car's origin, perhaps to intrigue and puzzle onlookers as much as anything. Fatty Arbuckle's Pierce-Arrow bore a radiator unlike any ordinary Pierce, and carried the film star's initials instead of the car's name. Pierces and other makes were disguised by the New York coachbuilders Brooks-Ostruk, and so were Cadillacs by Inglis P. Uppercu. There were two main categories of coachbuilt body: those designed by the bodybuilder, sometimes in conjunction with the chassis maker, and built in a small series; and the genuine custom job which was built to the purchaser's instructions. These would often take several

A classic disguised: the Brooks-Ostruk body is on a 1917 Pierce-Arrow chassis

months in construction, with frequent visits by the coachbuilder to the customer's home. Sometimes a particular hobby or enthusiasm would be reflected in the interior, such as the incredible Louis XVI décor in the Clark-bodied Rolls-Royce of 1927 ordered by Mr C. W. Gasque, a director of Woolworths.

The Depression inevitably thinned out the ranks of the wealthy buyers and, although classic cars and custom coachwork continued to be made, there was an undoubted decline in the quality and quantity of the top-grade cars. Duesenberg, the classic make *par excellence*, ceased production in 1937, and other American classics to disappear during the 1930s included Stutz, Pierce-Arrow, Cunningham and Franklin. There was still the occasional flash of originality such as the Phantom Corsair built by Rust Heinz, which was itself based on another classic, the Model 810 Cord (see page 85).

At the end of the Second World War it seemed there was little chance for the revival of the luxury car as it had been known in earlier days. Several countries had introduced penal taxation on high incomes, and France had also imposed a car tax which fell very heavily on anything over 3 litres' capacity. Some makes such as Hispano-Suiza never came back, but others announced new models one by one, so that by the 1950s there was a good selection for the wealthy buyer. The Rolls-Royce Silver Wraith was derived from the smaller of their pre-war models, the six-cylinder Wraith, but the engine was gradually increased in size, and with the introduction of the long-wheelbase model in 1952 imposing custom coachwork could again be made. The post-war coachbuilt era did not last beyond the 1950s in Britain, largely because the wages of skilled craftsmen were making the cars prohibitively expensive. Hooper, one of the great names in British coachbuilding since 1805, closed their doors in 1959, and a few years later the only coachbuilders were Mulliner and Park Ward, both subsidiaries of Rolls-Royce and therefore building only for that make. In the United States Derham struggled on alone through the 1950s, and even then their work was limited to customized interiors for standard bodies.

However, as the custom-bodied limousine was in the process of fading out a new kind of car appeared at the top end of the market. This was the GT (Gran Turismo) coupé, a two-door closed car, sometimes with two seats, sometimes four. Italy was the birthplace of the GT coupé, the

The Cunningham appealed to wealthy, conservative buyers.
This is a 1927 touring car

two best-known makes being Ferrari and Maserati, although there were some attractive smaller coupés by Fiat, Cisitalia and Abarth. The GT concept took a new direction when European manufacturers turned to American engines for their motive power, since these were cheaper to buy and easier to maintain. Examples of these new Euro-American hybrids were the British Gordon-Keeble, French Facel Vega, Italian Iso Rivolta and Grifo, and Swiss Monteverdi. Racing engines moved to a behind-the-driver position in the late

One of the first of the new generation of Euro-American GT coupés, the Gordon-Keeble of 1965

1950s, and this trend was reflected a few years later on mid-engined GT cars such as the Lamborghini Miura, Ferrari Dino and de Tomaso Mangusta and Pantera. The ultimate in such designs are the Ferrari Berlinetta Boxer and the Lamborghini Countach, both capable of nearly 200 mph and costing over £16,000. It is unlikely that any future road car will be as fast, for these cars were conceived just before the fuel crisis hit the world at the end of 1973.

The state limousine or landaulette is still made

A mid-engined GT coupé, this is a 1971 Ferrari Dino

in very limited numbers, more for monarchs and presidents than for private individuals. The very limited production of such cars is reflected in their cost; while the Rolls-Royce Phantom VI limousine is expensive enough at £44,000, the state landaulette on the same chassis costs over £50,000. The future of the classic car is hard to predict; it is not likely that there will be a large market for cars that are expensive to buy and to run, and the prospect for firms like Ferrari, Maserati and Aston Martin is hardly rosy. Perhaps the future lies in very limited production of individualistic cars such as Panther's de Ville, aimed at sales of no more than thirty to forty per year. If profits can be made with production figures as low as this. the buyers will doubtless be found, and even today there are a few buyers to whom price is a distinctly secondary consideration.

A fine example of a modern classic, the Rolls-Royce Camargue, one of the world's most expensive cars at a price. at the time of writing, of £37,539

1903 Mercedes (D)

Limousine

The 60 hp Mercedes introduced in 1903 set the standard by which high-class cars were judged, and its design was copied in many countries. Like other large cars of its day it was very versatile; in stripped two-seater form it won the Gordon Bennett race, and at the same time it could carry luxurious limousine coachwork like the car illustrated. In modern terms it was a Formula 1 racing car and a Rolls-Royce Phantom VI combined! This touring limousine was specially built for Emil Jellinek, the Mercedes agent in Nice, who did so much to bring the car about in the first place. The twin rear tyres are unusual, even on a car as large as this. It spent many years mouldering in a garage at the Villa Mercedes in Nice, but when the Villa was demolished in the 1950s it was taken to the Mercedes-Benz Museum, where it can be seen today.

Engine: 4-cyl, 140×150 mm, 9,236 cc. Low-tension magneto, overhead inlet valves, side exhaust. 70 bhp
Transmission: 4-speed, chain drive, 50 mph
Chassis: channel-steel frame, rear-wheel brakes

1905 C.G.V. (F)
limousine

The C.G.V. company was founded by three French racing drivers, Fernand Charron, Léonce Girardot and Emile Voigt. Their cars showed Panhard influence in the flitch-plate frames and automatic inlet valve engines, but they had Renault-style bonnets. Unlike Renaults, however, C.G.V.s carried their radiators below the front of the bonnet between the dumb irons. By 1905 they were making three large 4-cylinder models, of 4.9 6.2, and 9.8 litres' capacity. The car illustrated i one of the 'small' models with a limousine bod by Hooper of London.

Engine: 4-cyl, 110×135 mm, 4,942 cc. High tension magneto, side valves, 25 bhp
Transmission: 4-speed, chain drive, 35 mph
Chassis: armoured wood frame, rear-whee brakes. 12 ft 6 in wheelbase
Price: £640 (chassis only)

1907 Rolls-Royce (GB)
Tourer

The first Rolls-Royce model to receive international fame, the 40/50, was introduced in 1906 as a replacement for the 30 hp 6-cylinder car, which was among the least satisfactory Rolls models ever made. Its weakness lay in crankshaft vibration, and this was rectified in the 40/50 model, which had its cylinders cast in two blocks of three instead of three pairs. The car illustrated was the thirteenth chassis to be delivered, and was the original Silver Ghost, so called because of the colour of the body. The name has come to be applied to all the 40/50s made up to 1925, but

at the time the term 40/50 was generally used, both in advertising and by owners. Among the tests to which this particular car was subjected were a drive from Bexhill to Glasgow using only direct drive and overdrive top gears, and regular to-and-fro journeys from London to Glasgow totalling 15,000 miles. The car is still in existence, and is owned by Rolls-Royce Ltd.

Engine: 6-cyl, 114×114 mm, 7,036 cc. Dual ignition, side valves, 48 bhp
Transmission: 4-speed, shaft drive, 63 mph
Chassis: channel-steel frame, rear-wheel brakes. 11 ft 3½ in wheelbase
Price: £985 (chassis only)

1908 Napier (GB)

tourer

Some of the most remarkable cars ever seen have resulted from orders by Indian potentates in the days when their wealth was virtually unlimited. Napier was a popular choice of several Maharajahs, and its enormous 120 hp engine was capable of carrying even the most exotic coachwork ordered. This car was delivered to 'an Indian client' (the name was not recorded) in December 1908. It was 21 feet long, and could carry eleven passengers on its four rows of seats. A later example of a Maharajah's car is the Lanchester illustrated on page 42.

Engine: 6-cyl, 156×127 mm, 13,829 cc. High-tension magneto, side valves, 120 bhp
Transmission: 3-speed, shaft drive, 55 mph
Chassis: channel-steel frame, rear-wheel brakes
Price: not known (standard chassis was £2,500)

1908 Stearns (USA)
tourer

The F. B. Stearns Company of Cleveland, Ohio entered the automobile market in 1899 with a light buggy with single-cylinder engine. They gradually increased the size of their cars until they reached their limit with the mammoth 13-litre 6-cylinder car illustrated. The engine was so long that the rear pair of cylinders was located under the scuttle rather than under the bonnet proper.

Few of these enormous and expensive cars were made, but one has survived, and can be seen in America at Harrah's Automobile Collection, Reno, Nevada.

Engine: 6-cyl, 134×127 mm, 13,000 cc. High-tension magneto, side valves, 90 bhp
Transmission: 3-speed, chain drive, 88 mph
Chassis: channel-steel frame, rear-wheel brakes. 10 ft 8 in wheelbase
Price: $6,250

1909 Brooke (GB)
'Swan car'

This extraordinary car was designed by R. N Mathewson, an Englishman resident in Calcutta so that the body and chassis were assembled in India. The car was then shipped to England where it was fitted with a 6-cylinder engine by J. W Brooke & Company of Lowestoft, Suffolk, who were well-known makers of marine engines and also of cars, although their car-building days were almost over by 1910. Among the features of the car was a horn with eight organ pipes and a keyboard, air being provided by the exhaust system The swan's beak opened and shut with a hissing sound, and water could even be forced out of the bird's nostrils by a compressed air cylinder Needless to say, only one car of this kind was made and Mr Mathewson took it back to India after it was completed.

Engine: 6-cylinder. High-tension magneto, side valves
Chassis: channel-steel frame, rear-wheel brakes
Price: not known

1911 Mercer (USA)
raceabout

Often regarded as America's first sports car, although the term was not used at the time, the Mercer Type 35 Raceabout was introduced in 1910. It was the most sporting of a range of Type 35s which included the Runabout, a much staider machine with windscreen, doors and hood, a touring car and a limousine. Compared with the sports cars that were appearing in Europe at this time, the Mercer's engine was an unsophisticated 4-cylinder unit, with side valves in the old-fashioned T-head layout, but its light weight and high gearing gave it a good performance. No windscreen was provided, but a monocle for the driver could be bolted to the steering column. The Type 35 Raceabout was made until 1914, when it was replaced by the L-head 22–70; this was a faster and more modern car, yet it never quite achieved the out-and-out sporting glamour of the old Type 35. In the photo, the racing driver Ralph de Palma is at the wheel, and next to him is the film star Dorothy Lane.

Engine: 4-cyl, 111×127 mm, 4,900 cc. High-tension magneto, side valves, 60 bhp

Transmission: 4-speed, shaft drive, 75 mph
Chassis: channel-steel frame, rear-wheel brakes. 9 ft 0 in wheelbase
Price: $2,600

1912 Benz (D)
tourer

In 1909 the Benz company of Mannheim built a special racing car called the 'Blitzen' (lightning) Benz, with an overhead valve 4-cylinder engine of 21.5-litres' capacity. Several were built, and the Blitzen twice took the World Land Speed Record, its best time being 131.72 mph, with Barney Oldfield at the wheel, in 1910. Cars of this size were not unknown for racing, but it was most unusual for such a machine to be catalogued among a company's road-going models, yet that is what Benz did for the 1912 season. The car illustrated was used by Field Marshal von Hindenburg, and later came to England where it had a long racing career at Brooklands up to 1930.

Engine: 4-cyl, 185×200 mm, 21,504 cc. High-tension magneto, overhead valves, 200 bhp
Transmission: 3-speed, chain drive, 105 mph
Chassis: channel-steel frame, rear-wheel brakes. 11 ft 10¾ n wheelbase
Price: 30,000 DM (chassis only)

1912 Delaunay-Belleville (F)
town car

Delaunay-Belleville made some of the highest-quality cars in pre-1914 France, particularly their 6-cylinder models which were introduced in 1908. The standard models ranged from a relatively modest 4.1 litres to a large 8 litres, but there was also a real monster in the shape of the SMT model with a capacity of nearly 12 litres. This was built to the order of the Tsar of Russia (the initials SMT stood for Sa Majesté le Tsar), and of the three built, two were delivered to him. The third remained in France, and came into the hands of the Chief Inspector of Finance. This is the car illustrated. Note the twin rear tyres and enormous searchlight.

Engine: 6-cyl, 134×140 mm, 11,846 cc. High-tension magneto, side valves, 70 bhp
Transmission: 4-speed, chain drive, 70 mph
Chassis: channel-steel frame, rear-wheel brakes. 13 ft 5 in wheelbase

1914/19 Stoewer (D)
limousine

The chassis of this enormous Model F Stoewer was built in 1914, and is believed to have been owned by the Kaiser, when it was fitted with an open tourer body. In 1919 it was brought to England, and the elaborate limousine body illustrated was built by Mulliners to the order of Miss Gladys Dillon, the well-known dancer. Among its fittings were a parquet floor, silver-inlaid vanity case, card table and cupboards. The Model F was the rarest Stoewer made, only twelve leaving the factory between 1912 and 1914.

Engine: 4-cyl, 140×140 mm, 8,600 cc. High-tension magneto, overhead valves, 100 bhp
Transmission: 4-speed, shaft drive, 80 mph
Chassis: channel-steel frame, rear-wheel brakes
Price: 20,000 DM (original tourer)

1916 Crane Simplex (USA)
tourer

Crane Simplex was formed from the union of two American quality makes of car: the Crane Motor Car Company, whose products had been refined but little-known, and the Simplex Automobile Company whose big 4-cylinder cars were well-known, fast but not particularly smooth. Launched in 1915, the Crane-Simplex marked a turning point in the Simplex Company, for it was a beautifully made machine, as luxurious and expensive as anything on the market. The example shown has a nautical body with portholes in the cowl, funnels for ventilation, brass fittings throughout and a brass propeller behind the spare wheels. The body was built by Holbrook who made several more like it.

Engine: 6-cyl, 111×160 mm, 9,210 cc. High-tension magneto ignition, side valves, 110 bhp
Transmission: 3-speed, shaft drive, 75 mph
Chassis: channel-steel frame, rear brakes
Price: $10,000

1916 Pierce-Arrow (USA)
roadster

The Model 66 was the largest car made by Pierce-Arrow, one of America's best-known quality cars. Introduced in 1911, it had a 6-cylinder engine of 13.5 litres' capacity, and ran on 37-inch tyres. Prices ranged from $5,850 to $7,300. In 1914 the famous fender-mounted headlamps were introduced, which were to become a characteristic feature of Pierce-Arrows up to the end of production in 1938. Not all Pierces had these, and the roadster illustrated is one whose owner specified conventional lights. An anachronistic feature was right-hand drive, which Pierce-Arrow did not give up until 1921.

Engine: 6-cyl, 127×178 mm, 13,500 cc. Dual ignition, side valves
Transmission: 3-speed, shaft drive, 90 mph
Chassis: channel-steel frame, rear-wheel brakes. 12 ft 3 in wheelbase
Price: $5,900

1917 Fageol (USA)
tourer

Built by Fageol Motors Company of Oakland, California, this was one of the largest cars ever made for sale in the world with a 6-cylinder engine of 13.5 litres' capacity. It was naturally very expensive and the makers did not intend to build more than fifty cars per year, but as it appeared in the same year that America entered the First World War, production was probably much less than this. A distinctive feature of this luxury car was a name plate in carved ivory which was illuminated when the headlamps were turned on. The door handles and the tops of the control levers were also of ivory. The bell on the off-side front wing was not a standard Fageol feature, but an optional accessory. The cars were not made after 1918, but the Company went on to become one of America's best-known builders of buses.

Engine: 6-cyl, 127×178 mm, 13,500 cc. High-tension magneto, side valves, 125 bhp
Transmission: 3-speed, shaft drive, 80 mph
Chassis: channel-steel frame, rear-wheel brakes. 12 ft 1 in wheelbase
Price: about $13,000

1919 Packard (USA)
speedster

In 1915 Packard introduced the first 12-cylinder car to be sold to the public. Known as the Twin Six it was made until 1923, during which time more than 35,000 were sold. This was far more than any of the other V-12s which were made at this time, for Packard started off a veritable craze for multi-cylinder cars among American manufacturers. Most Twin Sixes had fairly staid coachwork, tourer or limousine bodies predominating, but an exception was this rakish speedster by an unknown coachbuilder. Its style was perhaps inspired by the special racing car with 14.8-litre V-12 engine with which Ralph de Palma took a number of records at Daytona Beach in 1919.

Engine: 12-cyl, 76×120 mm, 6,534 cc. Dual ignition, side valves, 88 bhp
Transmission: 3-speed, shaft drive, 90 mph
Chassis: channel-steel frame, rear-wheel brakes

1920 British Ensign (GB)
tourer

Like the Leyland Eight, the British Ensign was launched at a time when an expanding market for really expensive cars was anticipated. The company had made smaller cars and commercial vehicles since before the First World War, but the 38.4 hp Six of 1919 was a completely new design with single overhead camshaft engine. It could be had either with artillery wheels as illustrated, or with better-looking wire wheels. Unfortunately the hoped-for market did not really exist, and wealthy buyers preferred to stick to familiar products such as Rolls-Royce and Daimler. The design was later equipped with Entz magnetic transmission by the American, J. L. Crown, and sold under the name Crown Magnetic or Crown Ensign, but even fewer of these found buyers than the original British Ensign.

Engine: 6-cyl, 102×140 mm, 6,600 cc. High-tension magneto, overhead valves, 90 bhp
Transmission: 3-speed, shaft drive, 85 mph
Chassis: channel-steel frame, rear-wheel brakes. 12 ft 4 in wheelbase
Price: £1,700 (chassis only)

1920 Daniels (USA)
limousine

Made in Reading, Pennsylvania, the Daniels was a high-quality American car which always had distinctive lines, whether as a limousine or as a racy-looking 'submarine speedster'. Up to the end of 1919 Daniels used Herschell-Spillman V-8 engines, but afterwards changed to a larger V-8 of their own make. Most Daniels bodies were built by the Keystone Vehicle Company, located just across the street from the Daniels factory.

Production lasted from 1915 until 1924, during which time some 2,000 cars were made. They carried no identification beyond the letter 'D' on the hubcaps.

Engine: 8-cyl, 89×133 mm, 6,630 cc. Coil ignition, side valves, 90 bhp
Transmission: 3-speed, snaft drive, 74 mph
Chassis: channel-steel frame. rear-wheel brakes. 11 ft 0 in wheelbase
Price: $6,000

1920 Pierce-Arrow (USA)
phaeton

In the early 1920s a rich customer could have almost any modifications he wished on a car, so that sometimes it became barely recognizable. An example of this was the Pierce-Arrow phaeton built for the film star Roscoe 'Fatty' Arbuckle The radiator was quite different from any Pierce ever made, and carried a badge with his initials – R.C.A. Headlamps, wheels and body were also custom made for Arbuckle, and just about the only regular Pierce-Arrow features were the engine and right-hand drive, the latter a point that made Pierce virtually unique among American cars in 1920. The body was designed by Harley Earl, later to become a General Motors stylist, and was built by the Don Lee Coach and Body Works of Los Angeles.

Engine: 6-cyl, 127×178 mm, 13,500 cc. Dual ignition, side valves
Transmission: 3-speed, shaft drive, 85 mph
Chassis: channel-steel frame, rear-wheel brakes. 12 ft 3 in wheelbase

1920 Porter (USA)
tourer

The Porter was one of several very expensive, high-quality cars built in America in the early 1920s in such small numbers that they never became at all well known. It was designed by Finlay Robertson Porter who had previously built the F.R.P. car and designed the famous T-head Mercer. For the Porter he designed a 4-cylinder overhead camshaft engine which was built by the makers, The American and British Manufacturing Corp. of Connecticut. Some of America's finest coachbuilders, including Brewster, Demarest and Holbrook built a variety of open and closed bodies on the Porter chassis, but only thirty-four cars were made during a five-year period.

Engine: 4-cyl, 120×159 mm, 7,193 cc. Coil ignition, overhead valves, 140 bhp
Transmission: 4-speed, shaft drive, 90 mph
Chassis: channel-steel frame, rear-wheel brakes, 11 ft 10 in wheelbase
Price: about $10,200

1921 Cadillac (USA)
town car

More significant in the long run than Packard's V-12 was the V-8 engine which Cadillac introduced in 1914, for this layout was eventually to become standard for all large model American cars. Most designers moved up from four to six cylinders, but Cadillac's Wilfred Leland figured that eight would give even smoother power than six, so there has never been a 6-cylinder Cadillac. Although not the world's first V-8, the Cadillac was the first successful one, and the first to sell in large numbers. More than 13,000 were sold in 1915, the first full year of production, and by 1921, the year of the car illustrated, over 118,000 had been made. Note the absence of any windscreen on the stylish town car.

Engine: 8-cyl, 79×130 mm, 5,098 cc. Coil ignition, overhead valves, 76 bhp
Transmission: 3-speed, shaft drive, 75 mph
Chassis: channel-steel frame, rear-wheel brakes. 11 ft 2 in wheelbase

1921 Chitty-Bang-Bang (GB)
tourer

Just after the First World War there was quite a vogue for the building of fast cars with aircraft engines, which could be obtained for as little as £30 second hand. The most famous of these cars were undoubtedly the Chitty-Bang-Bangs built by Count Louis Zborowski at his country home in Kent in 1921 and 1922. Chitty I had a 23-litre Maybach engine and was raced quite a lot at Brooklands, while Chitty II, the car illustrated, had a four-seater tourer body, a smaller Benz engine of 'only'

18 litres, and raced but once at Brooklands. Like Chitty I, her chassis was that of a pre-war chain-drive Mercedes. Zborowski used Chitty II for long-distance touring, including a journey to the Sahara desert in 1922. This car still exists today, the only survivor of the three Chittys built.

Engine: 6-cyl, 145×190 mm, 18,882 cc. High-tension magneto, overhead valves, 230 bhp
Transmission: 4-speed, chain drive, 115 mph
Chassis: channel-steel frame, rear-wheel brakes
Price: not made for sale

1921 Leyland (GB)
Tourer

The Leyland Eight of 1920 to 1923 was the only passenger-car venture of the famous commercial-vehicle manufacturer from Lancashire. It was designed by J. G. Parry Thomas, who drove racing derivatives of the car with great success at Brooklands, and at the time when it was launched was the most powerful (145 bhp) and most expensive car on the British market. Among the advanced features of Thomas's design were a single overhead camshaft, torsion-bar rear suspension and vacuum-assisted brakes. The chassis came in three wheelbase lengths, and unlike most expensive cars of that time the Leyland could be had complete from the factory with their own bodywork, as illustrated. Closed bodies were made by specialist coachbuilders such as Maythorn or Windover. Only 18 Leyland Eights were made.

Engine: 8-cyl, 89×146 mm, 7,266 cc. Coil ignition, overhead valves, 145 bhp
Transmission: 4-speed, shaft drive, 90 mph
Chassis: channel-steel frame, 4-wheel brakes. 11 ft 9 in wheelbase
Price: £2,700

1922/23 Lanchester (GB)
racing cars

It has been said that almost every make of car was raced at Brooklands at one time or another and although Lanchester was never renowned as a sporting make, several examples ran there during the 1920s. The unusual-looking cars illustrated here were based on a 1911 25 hp chassis, fitted in 1922, with a very narrow tandem-seated racing saloon body. This in itself was most unusual for hardly any other enclosed Brooklands cars were ever built. Nicknamed 'Hoieh-wayaryeh-gointoo', designed and built by Tommy Hann, this car had ducts on either side of the seats through which the exhaust gases passed, leading to an opening in the tail of the car. It had some success during 1922, but in the following year Hann converted it to an open single-seater which he renamed 'Softly-catch-monkey'. This was raced at Brooklands during 1923 and 1924.

Engine: 4-cyl, 102×102 mm, 3,257 cc. High-tension magneto, overhead valves, 100 bhp
Transmission: 3-speed, shaft drive, 85 mph
Chassis: channel-steel frame, rear-wheel brakes 10 ft 7 in wheelbase

SOFTLY-CATCH-MONKEY"

1922 McFarlan (USA)
sedan

The McFarlan from Connersville, Indiana was a quality car made in small numbers from 1910 to 1928. Production never exceeded 235 cars per year, and in many years it was less than that. The company's most striking model was the TV Six, introduced in 1921. This had a large 6-cylinder engine with four valves per cylinder and triple ignition (two magnetos and a coil) needing eighteen sparking plugs. A variety of bodies was offered, of which the most striking was the Knickerbocker cabriolet, an ornate town car. The photograph shows a seven-passenger Suburban Sedan which was owned at one time by boxer Jack Dempsey.

Engine: 6-cyl, 114.3×152.4 mm, 9,380 cc. Triple ignition, overhead valves, 120 bhp
Transmission: 3-speed, shaft drive, 76 mph
Chassis: channel-steel frame, rear-wheel brakes. 11 ft 8 in wheelbase
Price: $7,800

1923 Delage (F)
tourer

The Delage Company was best known in the 1920s for its 2-litre DE and DI series of high-quality sports and touring cars, but they also made larger cars, the top of the range being the 6-litre GL series which was in the same class as the Hispano-Suiza. These large 6-cylinder cars with single overhead camshaft engines, twin oil pumps and hydraulic servo brakes were made in small numbers up to 1927. The car illustrated has an English body by Grahame-White of Hendon, Middlesex.

Engine: 6-cyl, 95×140 mm, 5,973 cc. High-tension magneto, overhead valves, 85 bhp
Transmission: 4-speed, shaft drive, 80 mph
Chassis: channel-steel frame, four-wheel brakes. 12 ft 8 in wheelbase
Price: £1,175 (chassis only)

1923 Farman (F)

coupé de ville

One of a crop of new makes of luxury car to appear in France after the First World War, the Farman was the product of the brothers Henry and Maurice Farman who were among the leading builders of aircraft during the war. Their cars had 6-cylinder engines with single overhead camshafts, a feature shared by the better-known Hispano-Suiza, but unlike the Hispano, they had four-speed gearboxes. From the start they had four-wheel brakes, of the 'Perrot-Waseige' system (Charles Waseige was the Farman's designer). A wide variety of bodies were built on the Farman chassis, not only by outside coachbuilders but also by Farman's own bodyworks. It was unusual for a luxury car maker to build their own bodies at this time. Farman production was very limited, and not more than 120 cars left the factory during eleven years of manufacture.

Engine: 6-cyl, 100×140 mm, 6,694 cc. High-tension magneto, overhead valves, 105 bhp
Transmission: 4-speed, shaft drive, 85 mph
Chassis: channel-steel frame, four-wheel brakes. 11 ft 9 in wheelbase
Price: 89,000 francs (chassis only)

1923 Locomobile (USA)
town car

The Locomobile was a conservative, high-quality American car of which the largest model, known as the Model 48, or Series VIII, underwent little change from its introduction in 1911 to the end of production in 1929. Its slogan, 'An Exclusive Car for Exclusive People', was justified by a production rate of only two per day in 1923, and prices started at $9,500 for a roadster and ran up to more than $13,000 for the custom-bodied cars such as this town car. Front-wheel brakes were announced in December 1923, costing $350 extra on a new car, or $450 if the owner returned his existing car to the factory to be modernized. This was quite often done with a car as expensive as a Locomobile. Note the front bumpers, which were rare at this date.

Engine: 6-cyl, 114×140 mm, 8,700 cc. High-tension magneto, side valves, 95 bhp
Transmission: 3-speed, shaft drive, 80 mph
Chassis: channel-steel frame, rear-wheel brakes. 11 ft 10 in wheelbase
Price: about $13,500

1924 Cadillac (USA)
limousine

Most buyers of Cadillac had been quite happy to
retain the standard radiator, but a small number in
the 1920s who wanted something more individual
were catered for by the New York City Cadillac
distributor, Inglis P. Uppercu. He not only built
custom bodies, but added his own design of
nickel radiator, which gave the cars a distinctive
appearance. They were known as Uppercu Cadillacs or sometimes simply as Uppercus, although

mechanically they were identical to the standard
models. In addition to passenger cars, Uppercu
made a small number of bus bodies on a length-
ened chassis.

Engine: 8-cyl, 79×130 mm, 5,098 cc. Coil
ignition, overhead valves, 76 bhp
Transmission: 3-speed, shaft drive, 75 mph
Chassis: channel-steel frame, rear-wheel brakes.
11 ft 2 in wheelbase
Price: about $4,000

1924 Cunningham (USA)
dual-cowl phaeton

The Cunningham from Rochester, New York was a car greatly respected by the more conservative American motorist who wanted a car more individual than a Packard or Cadillac, yet shunned the ostentation of a Duesenberg. Cunningham introduced their own design of V-8 engine in 1916, and employed this until passenger-car production was phased out in the early 1930s. Hearses were made for a few years longer. A wide variety of options were available to Cunningham clients, and wheels could be either wire, disc or artillery, with no variation in price. Although it was by no means a sports car, the phaeton illustrated has a number of 'sporty' features popular at the time, including cycle-type wings, step plates instead of running boards, and a separate windscreen for rear-seat passengers.

Engine: 8-cyl, 95×127 mm, 7,200 cc. Coil ignition, side valves, 100 bhp
Transmission: 4-speed, shaft drive, 90 mph
Chassis: channel-steel frame, four-wheel brakes. 11 ft 0 in wheelbase
Price: $6,400

1924 Lanchester (GB)
state landau

The Lanchester Forty was the senior of the two-model range which the Lanchester company of Birmingham offered in the 1920s. With a 6.6-litre single overhead camshaft engine it was a true luxury car, and a worthy rival to the Rolls-Royce Silver Ghost and Phantom 1. Several Forties were sold to India but none had such an elaborate body as this State Landau built for the Maharajah of Alwar. The body could be fully opened in fine weather, and was suspended on the chassis on large C-springs. This was in addition to the car's normal rear suspension. This magnificent machine is still in existence today.

Engine: 6-cyl, 101.6×127 mm, 6,178 cc. Dual ignition, overhead valves, 95 bhp
Transmission: 3-speed, shaft drive, 65 mph
Chassis: channel-steel frame, rear-wheel brakes. *c.* 14 ft 0 in wheelbase

1925 Doble (USA)
coupé

The only steam car which can, without fear of contradiction, be called a classic is the Doble, designed by Abner Doble and made in very small numbers at Emeryville, California. He had made some cheaper steam cars called Doble-Detroit, but when the Model E appeared in 1923 it was a machine of the highest quality, and with a performance hitherto unknown in steamers, which were in fact a dying breed in the 1920s. The Model E could accelerate from 0 to 40 mph in 8 seconds and, most important, it could move off in less than 40 seconds from starting up, whereas its contemporary, the Stanley, took half an hour. Many Dobles were fitted with coachwork by Murphy of Pasadena, which added expense to an already very costly chassis, so that the final price for a complete car could be as high as $12,000. Only about forty-five of the Model E and its successor, the Model F, were made between 1923 and 1932.

Engine: 4-cyl, 66.67×114×127 mm, 150 bhp
Transmission: direct drive, 95 mph
Chassis: channel-steel frame, four-wheel brakes. 11 ft 10 in wheelbase
Price: $10,000

1925 Wasp (USA)
rickshaw phaeton

Like the Porter, the Wasp was an expensive car built in very limited numbers. Between 1919 and 1925 only eighteen cars emerged from Karl H. Martin's small factory at Bennington, Vermont. Most of them used a 4-cylinder Wisconsin engine, but the last few had a 6-cylinder Continental unit. The car illustrated is one of these but, although the chassis was completed in 1925, the owner died before the body was finished so that the car did not run as a complete unit until 1961. An unusual feature of Wasp cars was the St Christopher medallion which was mounted on the dashboard as standard equipment.

Engine: 6-cyl, 92×133.3 mm, 5,335 cc. Coil ignition, side valves, 70 bhp
Transmission: 4-speed, shaft drive, 72 mph
Chassis: channel-steel frame, rear-wheel brakes. 12 ft 0 in wheelbase
Price: $4,500

1925 Voisin (F)

Tourer

Like Farman, Voisin was a new make introduced after the First World War, also produced by a firm well-known during the war for their aircraft. Gabriel Voisin's first car was originally planned as a large Citroën, but when that company decided to concentrate on small cars, the 4-litre sleeve-valve design was put on to the market as the Type C1 Voisin. It was made with little change until 1927, being supplemented with smaller 4-cylinder cars, and finally replaced by a 6-cylinder car of 2.3 litres' capacity. Voisins were bought by many celebrities including Rudolph Valentino, who had two, Anatole France, Josephine Baker and Maurice Chevalier. The car illustrated has a body by the British coachbuilders, Jarvis & Sons Ltd of Wimbledon.

Engine: 4-cyl, 95×140 mm, 3,969 cc. High-tension magneto, sleeve valves, 100 bhp
Transmission: 4-speed, shaft drive, 75 mph
Chassis: channel-steel frame, four-wheel brakes. 10 ft 11½ in wheelbase
Price: £830 (chassis only)

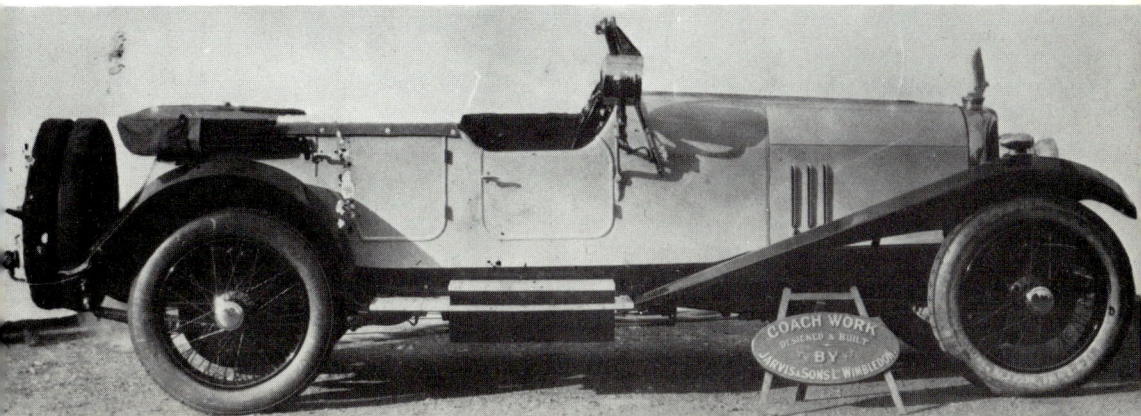

COACH WORK
DESIGNED & BUILT
BY
JARVIS & SONS L. WIMBLEDON

1926 Bugatti (F)
tourer

The Bugatti Royale was born of Ettore Bugatti's ambition to build a car surpassing the best that the world had seen in quality, size and performance. As originally built, it had a straight-8 engine of nearly 15 litres' capacity (production cars were slightly smaller at 12,763 cc), and a wheelbase of 14 ft 2 in. The first Royale, which was completed in the summer of 1926, had a simple open-tourer body from a Packard as illustrated, but this was later replaced by several other closed styles, ending up as an elegant sedanca de ville which still exists. Five other Royales were made, between 1928 and 1933, but despite the name, and presumably Bugatti's hopes, no royal person ever bought one. The price of a coupé at the Olympia Motor Show in 1932 was £6,500, that is, more than double that of the contemporary Rolls-Royce. Among many claims to uniqueness, the Royale has a hundred per cent survival rate; of the six made four are in the United States and two in France.

Engine: 8-cyl, 125×150 mm, 14,726 cc. Dual magneto, overhead valves, 250 bhp
Transmission: 3-speed, shaft drive, 120 mph
Chassis: channel-steel frame, four-wheel brakes, 14 ft 2 in wheelbase
Price: (1932) £6,500

1927 Lincoln (USA)
coaching brougham

The Lincoln has been the luxury product of the Ford Motor Company for so long that many people forget that it was once an independent make, sponsored by Henry Leland who had been with Cadillac. He launched the Lincoln V-8 in 1921 but ran into financial difficulties the following year, and his company was acquired by Ford. The same basic design was continued until 1932, the only alterations being the substitution of aluminium pistons in 1922 and an increase of capacity from 5.8 to 6.3 litres in 1928. The car shown has a highly individual special body in the style of a horse-drawn coach, made by the John B. Judkins Company of Merrimac, Massachusetts.

Engine: 8-cyl, 85.7×127 mm, 5,850 cc. Coil ignition, side valves, 95 bhp
Transmission: 3-speed, shaft drive, 80 mph
Chassis: channel-steel frame, four-wheel brakes. 11 ft 4 in wheelbase

1927 Rolls-Royce (GB)

sedanca de ville

The Rolls-Royce Phantom I, or New Phantom as it was generally called at the time, was introduced in 1925 as a replacement for the Silver Ghost which had been made since 1907. The engine was still a 6-cylinder, but now had overhead valves. The car illustrated has a most unusual and indeed unique body built by the Wolverhampton coach-builders, Clark. The interior is entirely fitted out in the style of Louis XVI, the panels and ceiling are painted with cherubs. The upholstery is Aubusson *petit point* and took nine months to make at a cost of £600. The companions at either side of the rear seat are of Battersea enamel.

Engine: 6-cyl, 108×140 mm, 7,668 cc. Dual ignition, overhead valves, 95 bhp
Transmission: 4-speed, shaft drive, 70 mph
Chassis: channel-steel frame, four-wheel brakes, 12 ft 6 in wheelbase
Price: about £3,600

1928 Isotta-Fraschini (I)
cabriolet

The Isotta-Fraschini was the first production car to have an eight-in-line engine, a fashion later followed by many manufacturers on both sides of the Atlantic. The Isotta was the most luxurious and, apart from the short-lived Super-Fiat, the biggest Italian car made in the vintage period, and was usually bracketed with the Rolls-Royce and Hispano-Suiza in a trio of European luxury cars.

Originally of 5.9 litres, the engine was enlarged to 7.4 litres in the Tipo 8A, made from 1925 to 1931. This is an 8A with two-seater cabriolet body by Gustav Nordberg of Stockholm, Sweden.

Engine: 8-cyl, 95×130 mm, 7,370 cc. High-tension magneto, overhead valves, 110 bhp
Chassis: channel-steel frame, four-wheel brakes. 11 ft 2½ in wheelbase
Price: £1,750 (chassis only)

1929 Duesenberg (USA)
sedan

The Model J Duesenberg is the epitome of American classicism, being a car of outstanding performance, and one of which nearly all models are of above-average appearance. Although Duesenberg cars had been on the market since 1920, it was the takeover of the company by Erret Lobban Cord in 1926 which pushed it into the limelight and gave birth to the Model J. With an output of 265 bhp from its twin overhead camshaft straight-8 engine, this was by far the most powerful car in America, and sold at a correspondingly high price. The original Model J was supplemented in 1932 by the supercharged Model SJ, which gave a claimed 320 bhp from the same sized engine. About 470 J-series Duesenbergs were made in all, of which not more than thirty-six were SJs. The photo shows an early Model J with Murphy sport sedan body.

Engine: 8-cyl, 95×121 mm, 6,882 cc. Coil ignition, overhead valves, 265 bhp
Transmission: 3-speed, shaft drive, 100 mph
Chassis: channel-steel frame, four-wheel brakes, 11 ft 10½ in wheelbase
Price: $12,500

1929 Stutz (USA)
roadster

The Stutz Bearcat had been one of the two great American speedsters of the 'teens and early 'twenties, but by 1925 the demand for cars with big 4-cylinder engines that put performance before comfort was nil, and the Stutz company had to find another image if they were to stay in business. The Stutz President, Frederick E. Moskovics, favoured a car with European standards of performance and road-holding, and yet one which yielded to no American make in silence and quality. Thus was born the Stutz Vertical Eight, with single overhead camshaft straight-8 engine, and an underslung worm final drive that made it the lowest car on American roads when it appeared in 1926. Many Stutz Vertical Eights had Weymann sedan bodies, but roadster models were also made, such as the LeBaron-bodied example illustrated. With four-seater bodies, Stutz had a distinguished career at Le Mans in 1928 and 1929, one leading Barnato's Speed Six Bentley for many hours in the 1928 event.

Engine: 8-cyl, 85.7×114.3 mm, 5,277 cc. Coil ignition, overhead valves, 113 bhp

Transmission: 4-speed, shaft drive, 90 mph
Chassis: channel-steel frame, four-wheel brakes. 11 ft 2½ in wheelbase.

1930 Burney Streamline (GB)
saloon

Sir Dennistoun Burney was the designer of the airship, R.100, and he was much concerned with aerodynamic shape as well as good weight distribution in the cars that he built at Maidenhead in the years 1930 to 1933. Only twelve were made, since Burney was more interested in experiment than in establishing a commercially successful manufacturing company. All were rear-engined, carrying their power units behind the rear axle which gave them a tail-heavy appearance, and in terms of present-day experience made for weight distribution that was far from ideal. The prototype had a 4-cylinder Alvis engine, but the 'production' model illustrated was powered by a 3-litre, straight-8 Beverley-Barnes unit. Other engines used in individual Burneys included Armstrong-Siddeley and the American Lycoming Six. One Burney was bought by the then Prince of Wales, later King Edward VIII and then Duke of Windsor.

Engine: 8-cyl, 66×108 mm, 2,956 cc. Coil ignition, overhead valves, 80 bhp
Transmission: 4-speed, spur gear drive, 70 mph

Chassis: channel-steel frame with girders supporting body, four-wheel brakes. 12 ft 5 in wheelbase
Price: £1,500

1930 Daimler (GB)
sports tourer

The 12-cylinder Daimler Double Six was usually clothed with formal limousine or landaulette coachwork, several of which were supplied to the British Royal Family. In 1930 a sporting model was prepared by Thompson & Taylor Ltd at Brooklands. This had a lowered chassis, so low that the top of the radiator was level with the mudguards. Only two of these low-chassis Double Sixes were made: the open car illustrated, and a

two-door saloon which was later converted to a drop-head coupé. The latter still exists. Fuel consumption of these cars was no better than 7.5 mpg, so they needed their enormous 46-gallon fuel tanks.

Engine: 12-cyl, 81.5×114 mm, 7,136 cc. Dual ignition, sleeve valves, 150 bhp
Transmission: 4-speed, shaft drive, 90 mph
Chassis: channel-steel frame, four-wheel brakes. 12 ft 3 in wheelbase

1930 Hispano-Suiza (F)
coupé

When the Hispano-Suiza H6 was announced in 1919 it caused a great sensation because of its combination of luxury and high performance. The original 6.6-litre single overhead camshaft six was supplemented by the 8-litre H6C in 1924, and the two were made up to 1934. The photograph shows an H6C with two-seater coupé body by Million-Guiet, a well-known French coachbuilder. These later H6Cs had less powerful engines than the first examples, so as to reduce engine noise — always more noticeable in the Hispano than in its principal rival, the Rolls-Royce

Engine: 6-cyl, 110×140 mm, 7,983 cc. Dual ignition, overhead valves, 144 bhp
Transmission: 3-speed, shaft drive, 100 mph
Chassis: channel-steel frame, four-wheel brakes. 11 ft 1 in wheelbase
Price: £1,950 (chassis only)

1930 Minerva (B)
phaeton

From 1900 to 1939 Minerva was one of the most respected names in the Belgian motor industry, and their top model in the classic era was the 40 hp Model AL straight-8. Made from 1930 to 1936, the AL was the larger of two straight-8s that Minerva launched at that time, the other being the 4-litre AP. The AL had dual ignition and a nine-bearing crankshaft. The domestic market for such a large and expensive car was very small, and quite a number of the hundred made were exported, particularly to the United States. The car shown has a phaeton body similar to that fitted to Model J Duesenbergs, made by Walter M. Murphy of Pasadena, California.

Engine: 8-cyl, 90×130 mm, 6,600 cc. Dual ignition, sleeve valves, 150 bhp
Transmission: 4-speed, shaft drive, 95 mph
Chassis: channel-steel frame, four-wheel brakes. 12 ft 9½ in wheelbase
Price: £1,200 (chassis only)

1930 Nacional Pescara (E)
roadster

The Nacional Pescara was sponsored by the Marqués Raoul Poteras de Pescara, and designed by his brother, Enrique, and Edmond Moglia. Some financial support came from the Spanish government, hence the 'nacional' part of the name; this doubtless flowed easier because King Alfonso XIII was a keen motoring enthusiast. The car had a twin-overhead camshaft straight-8 engine and was made in saloon and roadster form. Not many were made, for the King's exile in 1931 cut off the financial aid, and it is unlikely that the cars ever made a profit. Racing versions had some successes, including the 1931 European Mountain Championship. A projected straight-10 sports car was never built.

Engine: 8-cyl, 72.2×90 mm, 2,960 cc. Coil ignition, overhead valves, 75 bhp
Transmission: 3-speed, shaft drive, 100 mph
Chassis: channel-steel frame, four-wheel brakes. 9 ft 10 in wheelbase

1930 Ruxton (USA)
roadster

Similar in a number of ways to its contemporary, the Cord L-29, the Ruxton front-wheel-drive car was designed by William J. Muller and promoted by Archie M. Andrews, a director of the Hupp Motor Corporation. The engine was a Continental side-valve straight-8, and the bodies were built either by Budd (the sedans) or Raulang (the open models). The Ruxtons were actually put together in the factories of two other car makers, Moon and Kissel, and about five hundred were made before they both closed their doors, partly as a result of their involvement with the Ruxton venture. Competition from Cord was one cause of the Ruxton's downfall, but it was mainly the familiar story of trying to launch an unconventional car on insufficient capital at a time of economic depression.

Engine: 8-cyl, 76×120 mm, 4,405 cc. Coil ignition, side valves, 110 bhp
Transmission: 3-speed, front-wheel drive, 75 mph
Chassis: channel-steel frame, four-wheel brakes. 10 ft 10 in wheelbase
Price: $3,195

1931 Austro-Daimler (A)
limousine

As its name implies, Austro-Daimler began as the Austrian branch of the German company, but by the 1920s there were no longer any links in design between the two concerns. Austro-Daimler had the benefit of Ferdinand Porsche as chief designer for several years, and after he left in 1923 his assistant, Karl Rabe, took over. It was Rabe who was responsible for A-D's most distinctive feature in the late 1920s — their tubular-backbone frame which enclosed the propeller shaft, and was forked at the front to carry the engine. The model on which this was introduced was called the ADR, and could be had in touring form, as illustrated, or as a 100 bhp sports car. These were succeeded by the 3.6-litre ADR6 sports and 4.6-litre ADR8 straight-8 tourer.

Engine: 6-cyl, 76×110 mm, 2,994 cc. High-tension magneto, overhead valves, 70 bhp
Transmission: 4-speed, shaft drive, 75 mph
Chassis: tubular-backbone frame, four-wheel brakes. 11 ft 6½ in wheelbase
Price: 14,500 Rmk

1931 Bentley (GB)
coupé

The 8-litre Bentley was introduced towards the end of 1930 as a logical development of the 6½-litre model which had been made since 1925, these representing the 'carriage trade' end of the Bentley range, while the 4-cylinder 3- and 4½-litre cars were the sporting models. (Not that the 6½-litre was unsporting, for Speed Sixes won at Le Mans in 1929 and 1930.) With a capacity of 7,983 cc the 8-litre was the largest-engined British car of its day, and a chassis price of £1,850 took it into the Rolls-Royce class. Quite a number were made with limousine and sedanca-de-ville bodies, and it was just as good a town car as the Rolls Phantom II, some said better, but the latter had established itself as the epitome of the luxury car. Many customers for this class of car still thought of Bentley as a rather noisy sports car. Only one hundred 8-litres were sold before the makers went into receivership and were acquired by Rolls-Royce, who were naturally not keen to perpetuate a close rival to their own products.

Engine: 6-cyl, 110×140 mm, 7,983 cc. Dual ignition, overhead valves, 200 bhp

Transmission: 4-speed, shaft drive, 100 mph
Chassis: channel-steel frame, four-wheel brakes. 12 ft 0 in wheelbase
Price: £1,850 (chassis only)

1931 Cord (USA)
town car

Introduced in 1929, the Model L-29 Cord was the first car to bear the name of Erret Lobban Cord who had already been responsible for re-vitalizing the Auburn and Duesenberg companies. Designed by Cornelius van Ranst, the Cord's most distinctive feature was front-wheel drive, introduced at a time when this layout had hardly progressed beyond the experimental stage in any other cars. The engine was a Lycoming-built straight-8, and the car was the lowest and one of the most handsome of any on the American roads. Unfortunately the Depression hit sales, and anyway the American public were not overkeen on unusual designs, so that only 4,400 were made up to 1932. Most had Cord-designed bodies built by the Union City Body Company, but a number of custom coachbuilders on both sides of the Atlantic tried their hands on the L-29, including Murphy of Pasadena, Freestone & Webb of London, Maurice Proux of Paris and Castagna of Milan. The photograph shows a town car by Proux.

Engine: 8-cyl, 83×114 mm, 4,934 cc. Coil ignition, side valves, 125 bhp

Transmission: 3-speed, front-wheel drive, 77 mph
Chassis: channel-steel frame, four-wheel brakes. 11 ft 5½ in wheelbase
Price: $2,395 (stock sedan)

1931 Du Pont (USA)
phaeton

The Du Pont was a high-quality car made in small numbers from 1920 to 1932 by E. Paul Du Pont of the famous cellulose firm from Wilmington, Delaware. At first 4- and 6-cylinder models were made, but the make achieved its real fame with the Models G and H, powered by a straight-8 Continental engine, and made from 1928 to 1932. The Model G was one of the very few American cars to be raced at Le Mans, although Louis Miranda and Charles Moran's attempt in 1929 was not crowned with success; they were out of the race on the twentieth lap when ballast fell through the floor and broke the propeller shaft. The Model H was introduced in 1931, and was made in touring form rather than as a sports car. The Continental engine was mounted in a Stearns-Knight frame, and the cars were assembled in the Indian motorcycle factory at Springfield, Massachusetts. The photo shows a very handsome Model H with phaeton body by Locke.

Engine: 8-cyl, 85.7×114.3 mm, 5,274 cc. High-tension magneto, side valves, 125 bhp
Transmission: 4-speed, shaft drive, 90 mph

Chassis: channel-steel frame, four-wheel brakes. 12 ft 2 in wheelbase

1931 McLaughlin-Buick (CDN)
convertible sedan

Buicks were made in Canada under the name McLaughlin or McLaughlin-Buick from 1908 to 1942, and while most were almost identical to the US-built product, a number of specials were made, including several cars for royal visits as well as King Edward VIII's formal limousine of 1936. The car illustrated was built for a Toronto businessman, Winston Barron, in 1931 on the 8–90 chassis. The aluminium body was designed and built by the coachbuilders Smith Brothers of Toronto. The car, which has covered well over half a million miles, still exists today. Note the bonnet flutes, similar to those used by Vauxhall.

Engine: 8-cyl, 84×127 mm, 5,652 cc. Coil ignition, overhead valves, 104 bhp
Transmission: 3-speed, shaft drive, 85 mph
Chassis: channel-steel frame, front-wheel brakes, 11 ft 0 in wheelbase

1931 Peerless (USA)
sedan

The late 1920s saw two production 16-cylinder cars in America, the Cadillac and the Marmon. These inspired the Peerless Motor Car Company of Cleveland to follow suit, for their Sixes and Eights were selling none too well. Built in 1931 as a prototype for 1932 or 1933 models, the Peerless V-16 had an overhead-valve engine made largely of aluminium, and was designed by Fred W. Slack. Three engines were built, but only one complete V-16 car saw the light of day as the other two engines were tested in older chassis. The one complete car had a very handsome sedan body by Murphy, also largely of aluminium construction. An advanced feature of this car was that the doors opened into the roof. Unfortunately the company was on the verge of closure in 1931, and no further Peerlesses of any description were made. The one prototype survives, though, and can be seen in the Frederick C. Crawford Auto-Aviation Museum in Cleveland, Ohio.

Engine: 16-cyl, 82.5×89 mm, 7,610 cc. Coil ignition, overhead valves, 173 bhp
Transmission: 3-speed, shaft drive, 100 mph
Chassis: channel-steel frame, four-wheel brakes. 12 ft 1 in wheelbase
Price: never fixed

1931 Sunbeam (GB)

saloon

One of the most popular models from the Sunbeam Motor Car Company of Wolverhampton was the Twenty, whose RAC horse-power rating was in fact 23.8. It had a pushrod overhead-valve engine with seven main bearings, and its vintage ancestry was seen in such features as right-hand gearchange and non-synchromesh gearboxes. Many of the model Twentys, including the saloon illustrated, had Weymann bodies with fabric panelling over a flexible wooden frame. In 1932 there was a new model, the Speed Twenty, of more modern appearance than the 'ordinary' Twenty, but with an older engine, the 3-litre four-bearing unit left over from the 1920s. These Sunbeams were made until 1935 when the whole Sunbeam-Talbot-Darracq empire collapsed and was bought by the Rootes Group who introduced new and cheaper cars under the name Sunbeam-Talbot. The descendants of these were re-named Sunbeam in 1954.

Engine: 6-cyl, 80×110 mm, 3,317 cc. High-tension magneto, overhead valves
Transmission: 4-speed, shaft drive, 75 mph

Chassis: channel-steel frame, four-wheel brakes. 10 ft 4$\frac{1}{4}$ in wheelbase
Price: £750

1931 Walter (CS)
cabriolet

Walter was a medium-sized Czech company that made cars, lorries and aero engines, continuing the latter after vehicle production ceased in 1936. Most of their cars had 4- or 6-cylinder engines, and some were based on Fiats, but in 1931 Walter stepped out of line when they introduced a luxury chassis powered by a V-12 engine of nearly 6 litres' capacity. Known as the Royal, the design bore some resemblance to Maybach's V-12, and incorporated the Maybach *Doppelschnellgang*

8-speed gearbox. Only five were made, most of them four-door cabriolets similar to the one illustrated. This was built for Mr Tony Kumpera, owner of the Walter factory which was situated near Prague.

Engine: 12-cyl, 76×108 mm, 5,879 cc. Coil ignition, overhead valves, 120 bhp
Transmission: 8-speed, shaft drive, 85 mph
Chassis: channel-steel frame, four-wheel brakes. 11 ft 9½ in wheelbase
Price: 220,000 Kcs

1932 Bucciali (F)
saloon

The Bucciali brothers had inherited a fortune from their father who manufactured fairground equipment, so they were not unduly worried that their cars seldom, if ever, showed a profit. They began manufacture in 1923 with small sports cars powered by Violet 2-stroke engines, but in 1928 they turned to a series of front-wheel-drive cars with independent suspension all round and, some of them, with automatic transmission. These used 6- and 8-cylinder Continental engines, a Voisin sleeve-valve V-12 and, in the car illustrated, a 16-cylinder unit made up of two straight-8 Continental blocks mounted side by side on a common aluminium crankcase. The crankshafts were geared together. Only one of these cars was made, and it is said never to have run under its own power, although the chassis survives today.

Engine: 16-cyl, 72×120 mm, 7,820 cc. Coil ignition, side valves, 180 bhp
Transmission: 3-speed, shaft drive
Chassis: channel-steel frame, four-wheel brakes. 11 ft 8 in wheelbase
Price: 210,000 francs

1932 Bugatti (F)
Cabriolet

Since the Bugatti Royale could hardly be called a production car, the 5.3-litre straight-8 Type 46 was the largest production Bugatti made. It was intended for luxurious touring coachwork rather than as a sports car, although there was also a supercharged model, the 46S which had a highly satisfactory performance. Unlike most Bugattis, the Type 46 had a 3-speed gearbox which was in unit with the rear axle. Three speeds were also featured in the sporting and racing derivatives of the 46, the Types 50 and 54. The 46 was said to be Ettore Bugatti's favourite model. Over 400 were sold between 1929 and 1936, although customers were hard to find in the last few years, and three or four brand-new chassis were 'discovered' in the 1960s. The car illustrated has coachwork by Neuss of Germany, and was owned from 1932 to 1934 by Prince Gustav Adolf of Sweden.

Engine: 8-cyl, 81×130 mm, 5,359 cc. High-tension magneto, overhead valves
Transmission: 3-speed, shaft drive, 90 mph
Chassis: channel-steel frame, four-wheel brakes. 11 ft 6 in wheelbase
Price: £975 (chassis only)

1932 Franklin (USA)
Club Brougham

Most successful American cars have been conventional in design, but the Franklin was exceptional in two ways. Throughout the company's life (1901–34) they made only air-cooled cars, and until 1928 wooden frames were used. They were the last of the quality car makers to turn to four-wheel brakes, which did not come until 1928. Nevertheless Franklins were always well thought of, and several models of the late 1920s and early 1930s are undisputed classics. In 1932 they launched their V-12, which was made from April of that year until all production ceased in the early months of 1934. The photo shows a V-12 Club Brougham which was unchanged in appearance from 1932 to 1934.

Engine: 12-cyl, 82.5×107.5 mm, 6,810 cc. Coil ignition, overhead valves, 150 bhp
Transmission: 3-speed, shaft drive, 95 mph
Chassis: channel-steel frame, four-wheel brakes, 12 ft 0 in wheelbase
Price: $4,400 (in 1932)

1932 Maybach (D)
cabriolet

The Maybach was the grandest German car of the interwar period, and by reason of its limited production had a *cachet* which the better-known Mercedes-Benz never quite achieved. The Maybach Motorenwerke G.m.b.H. built aero engines, especially for Zeppelin airships, so that when they launched their 12-cylinder car in 1929, this too was called the Zeppelin. Originally made in 7-litre form, the engine was enlarged to 8 litres in 1931, and this was the classic Maybach Zeppelin made up to the outbreak of war in 1939. It was a massive machine with a bonnet length of seven feet and a weight of well over three tons in closed form. The *Doppelschnellgang* overdrive gave two low gears and three higher gears, the latter with two speeds each; the total number of ratios available was therefore eight forward and four reverse. Control was by levers on the steering wheel, and a floor lever. Some Zeppelins were fitted with striking aerodynamic bodywork by Spohn, but most were limousines or cabriolets. About 300 12-cylinder Maybachs were made.

Engine: 12-cyl, 92×100 mm, 7,977 cc. Coil ignition, overhead valves, 200 bhp
Transmission: 8-speed, shaft drive, 100 mph
Chassis: channel-steel frame, four-wheel brakes. 12 ft 3 in wheelbase
Price: 27,000 DM (chassis only)

1932 Miller (USA)

sports car

Harry Armenius Miller earned his fame by building some of the best-known and most successful American racing cars in the 1920s, and his road-going cars, of which he made only two, were very much a sideline. This car was just about the ultimate in sporting machinery, with a 4.9-litre V-8 engine with a single overhead camshaft to each block, and a boat-tailed aluminium body with a lid in the rear deck into which the hood could be folded. Miller went bankrupt before the car could be completed, and it was finished off by the J. Gerard Kirchoff Body Works in Pasadena, California. It is believed to have cost its millionaire owner, Philip Chancellor, $30,000.

Engine: 8-cyl, 86×105 mm, 4,965 cc. Coil ignition, overhead valves, 325 bhp
Transmission: 4-speed, front-wheel drive, 135 mph
Chassis: channel-steel frame, four-wheel brakes. 10 ft 0 in wheelbase
Price: about $30,000

1932 Reo (USA)
convertible coupé

For most of its car-making life Ransom E. Olds' Reo Motor Car Company concentrated on the low- to medium-priced class, but in 1931 they sought to enter the luxury market with the Custom Royale range. These cars had 5.9-litre straight-8 engines and coachwork designed by Count Alexis de Sakhnoffsky. They had automatic chassis lubrication and came in three wheelbase lengths, the longest of which, 12 ft 8 in, was reserved for the formal limousine style. Bodies were built by the Hayes Body Company of Grand Rapids, Michigan. The Custom Royale range was made from 1931 to 1934, after which Reo reverted to cheaper cars (which they had always made alongside the Royales). In 1936 they abandoned passenger car production altogether to concentrate on commercial vehicles.

Engine: 8-cyl, 85.7×127 mm, 5,810 cc. Coil ignition, side valves, 125 bhp
Transmission: 3-speed, shaft drive, 95 mph
Chassis: channel-steel frame, four-wheel brakes. 11 ft 3 in wheelbase
Price: $2,445 (sedan)

1933 Auburn (USA)
speedster

Auburn had been one of the staider American makes up to 1925, when Erret Lobban Cord's acquisition of the company was reflected in smarter lines and two-tone colour schemes. Up to 1932 the largest Auburn was a straight-8, but in that year the company announced its V-12, powered by a 6.4-litre Lycoming engine and selling for the remarkably low price of $975 for a two-passenger coupé. The rakish-looking speedster illustrated was naturally more expensive at $1,600 but even so it was priced well below rival V-12s, such as Cadillac and Lincoln. Unfortunately this modest price was counter-productive in two ways, for the company made little, if any, profit on each car, and many buyers felt that such a cheap V-12 could not possibly be a good V-12. After three seasons, the Auburn V-12 was dropped, and by the end of 1936 Auburn was no longer making cars at all.

Engine: 12-cyl, 79×108 mm, 6,417 cc. Coil ignition, side valves. 165 bhp
Transmission: 3-speed, shaft drive, 105 mph
Chassis: channel-steel frame, four-wheel brakes. 11 ft 1 in wheelbase
Price: $1,600

1933 Chrysler (USA)
dual-cowl phaeton

Chrysler introduced their Imperial line in 1926 with the Imperial 80, guaranteed to do 80 mph. It was the top line of the Chrysler range, and in 1931 became even more distinctive with the arrival of the long-wheelbase straight-8 CG series. These were among the best-looking Chryslers ever made, particularly when fitted with LeBaron coachwork. The 1933 models were the CQ and CL, with wheelbases of 10 ft 6 in and 12 ft 2 in respectively. The car illustrated is a CL with LeBaron body. The following year these handsome cars were replaced by the streamlined, but distinctly unhandsome, Airflow series. The most expensive Chryslers continued to bear the name Imperial, however, and in 1955 this became a separate make within the Chrysler Corporation.

Engine: 8-cyl, 89×127 mm, 6,304 cc. Coil ignition, side valves, 135 bhp
Transmission: 3-speed, shaft drive, 88 mph
Chassis: channel-steel frame, four-wheel brakes. 12 ft 2 in wheelbase
Price: $3,395

1933 Pierce-Arrow (USA)
sedan

The radically styled Pierce-Arrow 'Silver Arrow' was billed as 'giving you in 1933 the car of 1940', and certainly features like its recessed headlights and straight-through wing line were several years ahead of their time. The spare wheels were concealed in compartments behind the front wheels. The first 'Silver Arrow' was exhibited at the 1933 Chicago World's Fair, but it was more than a mere show car; four others were built and a production run planned, at a price of $10,000 each. Unfortunately the effects of the Depression and Pierce-Arrow's rather shaky financial state put paid to this scheme, although more conventional cars were made under the name 'Silver Arrow' in 1934 and 1935. These had a similar pointed tail, but a conventional wing line. The 1933 'Silver Arrow's' engine was the stock V-12 that Pierce were using in their larger models at that time.

Engine: 12-cyl, 89×101 mm, 7,572 cc. Coil ignition, overhead valves, 175 bhp
Transmission: 3-speed, shaft drive, 110 mph
Chassis: channel-steel frame, four-wheel brakes. 11 ft 7 in wheelbase
Price: $10,000

1933 Rohr (D)
saloon

The Rohr Company of Ober-Ramstadt built mainly cars with small straight-8 engines from 1928 to 1935, although they also made a few 4-cylinder cars under licence from the Czech Tatra Company. The striking streamlined saloon illustrated has a body specially built by Autenriet for the 1933 Berlin Motor Show. The chassis is a standard straight-8. Only one of this body-style was made and the car is now owned by Edgar E. Rohr (no relation to the car's builders) of Manassas, Virginia, USA.

Engine: 8-cyl, 70×108 mm, 3,287 cc. Coil ignition, overhead valves, 75 bhp
Transmission: 3-speed, shaft drive, 83 mph
Chassis: channel-steel frame, four-wheel brakes. 10 ft 8 in wheelbase

1934 Brewster (USA)
convertible sedan

Brewster & Company of Long Island City, New York, were one of America's oldest coachbuilders, with a history dating back to 1810. From 1915 to 1925 they built a high-quality smallish car of their own, in addition to coachwork on other people's chassis. There followed nine years when they concentrated mainly on bodies for the American Rolls-Royce, and in 1934 they again offered cars under their own name. This time they were Ford V-8-based, with Brewster's own distinctive bodies characterized by a curved radiator grille and dramatic down-pointing bumpers. Body styles included closed sedans and town cars, convertible sedans as illustrated, and a few roadsters with rumble seats. These cars cost up to $3,500, compared with $760 for the most expensive stock Ford V-8, but nevertheless about 300 found customers between 1934 and 1936.

Engine: 8-cyl, 77.79×95.25 mm, 3,622 cc. Coil ignition, side valves, 90 bhp
Transmission: 3-speed, shaft drive, 75 mph
Chassis: channel-steel frame, four-wheel brakes, 10 ft 7 in wheelbase
Price: $3,500

1935/38 Cadillac (USA)
convertible

Cadillac's V-16 was made in larger numbers than any other car with this number of cylinders, over 4,500 leaving the factory between 1930 and 1940. The standard models of the early 1930s were the epitome of American classicism, and among the most handsome cars of their era made anywhere in the world. Few people would accord such praise to the car illustrated, yet it is an interesting example of flamboyant streamlined European styling applied to a classic American car. On a 1935 V-16 chassis the little-known Swiss coachbuilder Hartmann of Lausanne built this convertible in 1938. The car, which was almost certainly a one-off, still exists, and was photographed at a Swiss rally in 1971.

Engine: 16-cyl, 76×101.5 mm, 7,420 cc. Coil ignition, overhead valves, 175 bhp
Transmission: 3-speed, shaft drive, 90 mph
Chassis: channel-steel frame, four-wheel brakes. 12 ft 4 in wheelbase

1935 Duesenberg (USA)
sports car

This striking car started life as a stock 1935 Duesenberg Model SJ, but its owner, Ab Jenkins, equipped it with dual carburettors and special manifolding, and mounted a lightweight stream-lined body. In this form the car took Class B international records of 152 mph for one hour and 135.47 mph for twenty-four hours. In 1936 Jenkins fitted a more powerful engine, a Curtiss Conqueror aircraft unit, and renamed the car the Mormon Meteor, since Salt Lake City, near the Bonneville Salt Flats where his records were made, is the headquarters of the Mormon faith.

With the aircraft engine further records were taken in 1936 and 1937, after which Jenkins, feeling the need for a completely new car for record work, re-installed the Duesenberg engine and ran the car regularly on the road for five years. The photograph shows it after it had been re-equipped for road use, and was probably taken shortly after the Second World War.

Engine: 8-cyl, 95×121 mm, 6,882 cc. Dual-coil ignition, overhead valves, 320 bhp
Transmission: 3-speed, shaft drive, 160 mph
Chassis: channel-steel frame, four-wheel brakes. 11 ft 10½ in wheelbase
Price: $10,000 (chassis only)

1935 Packard (USA)
Formal sedan

Packard was a pioneer of the V-12 engine, having made over 35,000 of their Twin Sixes between 1916 and 1923. In 1932 they returned to the 12-cylinder engine with the new Twin Six. These represented a very small part of Packard's total production, and each one carried a certificate from the racing driver Tommy Milton to the effect that he had driven it for 250 miles on the Packard speedway. In 1933 the name was changed to Packard Twelve, and the model was made until 1939. The car illustrated has a factory body, but many Twelves were given custom coachwork by such firms as LeBaron, Derham and Brunn.

Engine: 12-cyl, 87.3×108 mm, 7,686 cc. Coil ignition, side valves, 175 bhp
Transmission: 3-speed, shaft drive, 95 mph
Chassis: channel-steel frame, four-wheel brakes. 11 ft 7 in wheelbase
Price: $4,660

1935 Tatra (CS)
saloon

Although their predecessors, Nesselsdorf, had produced some expensive cars, Tatra made their reputation in the 1920s with the little 2- and 4-cylinder machines with tubular-backbone frame, which were made in larger numbers than any other cars in the Czechoslovak Republic. In 1931 they announced a car at the other end of the scale, the luxurious Type 80 with a 6-litre V-12 engine. The only feature that this shared with the little Tatras was the backbone frame. A total of twenty-five Type 80s were made over a five-year period, the saloon shown being one of the last and having more rounded lines than most. Coachwork included some cabriolets by Czechoslovakia's leading coachbuilder, Sodomka, and a landaulette for President Masaryk.

Engine: 12-cyl, 75×113 mm, 5,990 cc. Coil ignition, overhead valves, 120 bhp
Transmission: 4-speed, shaft drive, 85 mph
Chassis: tubular-backbone frame, four-wheel brakes. 12 ft 7 in wheelbase

1936 Squire (GB)

sports car

Like many schoolboys, Adrian Squire doodled designs of cars during lessons, but he was unusual in that within a few years of leaving school he was a car manufacturer in his own right. Announced in September 1934, the 1.5-litre Squire was a beautifully built and extremely expensive sports car, selling at between £1,220 and £1,245. This was at a time when a similar-sized Aston Martin cost £625 and a Frazer Nash between £475 and £550. Only seven Squires were sold, mostly to personal friends of the builder. The power unit was a twin-overhead camshaft supercharged Anzani engine, and among other quality features of the car were Marchal headlamps (on the prototype only) and massive brakedrums capable of stopping the car in 20 feet from 30 mph. Two wheelbase lengths were available, the car illustrated being the longer one with a four-seater Vanden Plas body. Supplied to Sir James Walker, this was the last Squire to leave the little factory at Henley-on-Thames.

Engine: 4-cyl, 69×100 mm, 1,496 cc. Coil ignition, overhead valves, 110 bhp
Transmission: 4-speed, shaft drive, 102 mph
Chassis: channel-steel frame, four-wheel brakes. 10 ft 3 in wheelbase
Price: £1,195

1937 Delage (F)
coupé

The Delage company had a history reaching back to 1906, and from 1920 onwards they had a reputation for cars which combined quality with exceptionally good looks. This was particularly true of the straight-8 models known as the D.8 series, introduced in 1929, and these were progressively developed during the next ten years, although the takeover of Delage by Delahaye in 1935 meant that the new generation of straight-8s followed Delahaye design to a great extent. Two versions were made, the D.8-100 and the D.8-120, the latter being the sporting version with 140 bhp engine. A feature of these Delages was the Cota electro-magnetic gearbox. Although they were not sports cars and played virtually no part in competitions (Delage's Le Mans cars were the 6-cylinder models), the D.8s were fitted with very handsome and sometimes sporting coachwork. The car illustrated has a coupé body by Le Tourneur et Marchand.

Engine: 8-cyl, 80×107 mm, 4,300 cc. Coil ignition. overhead valves, 140 bhp
Transmission: 4-speed, shaft drive, 94 mph
Chassis: channel-steel frame, four-wheel brakes, 11 ft 1 in wheelbase
Price: £1,050 (chassis only)

937/48 Delahaye (F)

oadster

ew companies had a more dramatic transforma-
on during the 1930s than Delahaye, who began
he decade with a range of remarkably dull cars,
oth in appearance and performance, but with the
ntroduction of the 3.5-litre 6-cylinder Type 135
n 1936 they entered the ranks of luxury and
porting cars, in which they were to remain until
ar production ceased in 1954. In 1937 they built
 V-12 Grand Prix racing car, and from this was
eveloped the V-12 road car known as the Type
65. It had a 4.5-litre engine with the same cylinder
imensions as the Lagonda V-12, dry-sump
ubrication inherited from the racing engines, and a
ᴄotal gearbox. Some very flamboyant coachwork
vas available on the Type 165, with spatted
vheels at front and back. The car illustrated is in
act a Type 145 Grand Prix car, which was
ebodied by Franay in 1948 to the order of Prince
ᴿainier of Monaco. This car, which still exists
oday, is the only Type 145 to survive.

ᴱngine: 12-cyl, 75×84.5 mm, 4,480 cc. Mag-
ᴺeto ignition, overhead valves, 238 bhp
ᵀransmission: 4-speed, shaft drive, 115 mph

Chassis: channel-steel frame, four-wheel brakes.
10 ft 6 in wheelbase
Price: not for general sale

1937 Lincoln (USA)
convertible roadster

Lincoln was the prestige car of the Ford Motor Company, and their prestige never stood higher than in the years 1930 to 1948, when they made only 12-cylinder cars. Their top line was the K Series, which had 6.8-litre engines with aluminium cylinder heads and dual-coil ignition. In 1937 the headlamps were faired into the wings as on the car illustrated, and limited production of these big cars continued until 1939, although the last ones made were sold off in 1940. By this time the bulk of Lincolns made were the smaller and cheaper Zephyrs with 4.3- or 4.8-litre V-12 engines, and from these were derived the famous Continental made from 1940 to 1948, and sometimes called 'instant classics'. Be that as it may, they were not the equal of the big K Series. The car illustrated has a roadster body by LeBaron, a rare style of which only fifteen were made in 1937.

Engine: 12-cyl, 79.4×114.3 mm, 6,784 cc. Dual coil ignition, side valves, 150 bhp
Transmission: 3-speed, shaft drive, 90 mph
Chassis: channel-steel frame, four-wheel brakes 11 ft 4 in wheelbase
Price: $4,950

1937 Phantom Corsair (USA)
coupé

Few people are fortunate enough to be able to design and build their ideal car with a virtually free hand, but one such man was Rust Heinz, second son of millionaire H. J. Heinz. In 1936 he engaged the services of the Californian coachbuilders Bohman & Schwartz to build an ultra-streamlined coupé using a Cord V-8 engine and special chassis frame. The bench-type front seat could accommodate four passengers at a pinch, and there were also two almost uninhabitable seats at the rear. Door opening was by electric push-buttons, which meant that if the battery were dead you couldn't get into the car. Despite its 'dream car' character, the Phantom Corsair was intended for limited production, to sell at $14,700 each. Estimates for the cost of the prototype vary from $24,000 to $35,000. Unfortunately Heinz was killed in a car crash (not while driving the Corsair) in July 1939, and only the one car was ever made. It survives today in Harrah's Automobile Collection at Reno, Nevada.

Engine: 8-cyl, 89×95 mm, 4,730 cc. Coil ignition, side valves, 190 bhp
Transmission: 4-speed, front-wheel drive, 115 mph
Chassis: chrome-moly steel frame, four-wheel brakes. 10 ft 5 in wheelbase
Price: $14,700 (planned production models)

1938 Buick (USA)
town car

At first glance this car would seem to be a Rolls-Royce, but it is in fact a Buick Limited with body by the Paris coachbuilders Fernandez et Darrin who also made the radiator. This bears the name Fernandez et Darrin. Paris, so there is no external indication of the car's true identity. The only stock Buick parts visible are the head, tail and parking lights. Built for use in Paris, the car is now owned by Jim Robbins of Dearborn, Michigan, USA.

Engine: 8-cyl, 87.3×109.5 mm, 5,247 cc. Coil ignition, overhead valves, 141 bhp
Transmission: 3-speed, shaft drive, 90 mph
Chassis: channel-steel frame, four-wheel brakes. 11 ft 8 in wheelbase

1938 Hispano-Suiza (F)
coupé

The V-12 Hispano-Suiza was the last important design to emerge from the great French factory, being made from 1931 to 1939. It was built in two sizes, 9.4 litres and 11.2 litres, although only a few were made of the latter. Probably the most unusual body ever mounted on a V-12 chassis is the one illustrated, which was built to the order of André Dubonnet by the Paris coachbuilders, Saoutchik. It is of aluminium alloy, and the doors slide to open. Unlike most coachwork on Hispano chassis, it has Saoutchik's own design of bonnet and grille, which completely disguises the chassis make. Front suspension is independent, by Dubonnet's design of coil springs in oil-filled cylinders. The car's present owner is Monsieur Alain Balleret, president of le Club Hispano.

Engine: 12-cyl, 100×100 mm, 9,424 cc. Dual magnetos, overhead valves, 220 bhp
Transmission: 3-speed, shaft drive, 100 mph
Chassis: channel-steel frame, four-wheel brakes. 12 ft 2 in wheelbase

1938 Mercedes-Benz (D)
limousine

The best-known big Mercedes-Benz cars of the 1930s were the supercharged 500K and 540K series, but even bigger and more expensive were the 770Ks, known as the 'Grosser Mercedes'. The first series was introduced in 1930 and made in very limited numbers until 1937 when it was replaced by the second series, of which the limousine is illustrated. This used the same 7.7-litre straight-8 engine, but had a new tubular chassis in place of the channel frame of the first series, and independent suspension by four-coil springs in place of semi-elliptics. As well as the limousine there were several models of open cabriolet on the 770K chassis, and these were particularly favoured by Adolf Hitler and other members of the Nazi hierarchy. It has been suggested that the cars of the second series were never for sale to the general public, but were reserved for party officials or as gifts for foreign heads of state. Probably not more than twenty or thirty were made.

Engine: 8-cyl, 95×135 mm, 7,655 cc. Coil ignition, overhead valves, 155 bhp (230 bhp with supercharger)
Transmission: 4-speed, shaft drive, 110 mph
Chassis: tubular-steel frame, four-wheel brakes. 12 ft 10 in wheelbase
Price: not for general sale.

1939 Lagonda (GB)
drophead coupé

Apart from the Rolls-Royce Phantom III, the Lagonda V-12 was Britain's only 12-cylinder car made in the late 1930s. Introduced in 1937, its 4.5-litre engine was designed by W. O. Bentley who had joined Lagondas two years previously. Each block of cylinders had a single overhead camshaft, and there were twin distributors and twin carburettors. Three wheelbase lengths were available, and coachwork varied from the coupé illustrated, on the short wheelbase, to some formal limousines and sedanca de villes on the long 11 ft 6 in wheelbase. The V-12 was an ideal car for

long-distance, high-speed cruising, for its engine was better able to stand up to continuous high speeds than was that of its rival the $4\frac{1}{4}$-litre Bentley. Two V-12s, with lightweight bodies and tuned engines, ran at Le Mans in 1939, to finish 3rd and 4th. The V-12 was not revived after the war.

Engine: 12-cyl, 75×84.5 mm, 4,480 cc. Coil ignition, overhead valves, 180 bhp
Transmission: 4-speed, shaft drive, 108 mph
Chassis: channel-steel frame, four-wheel brakes. 10 ft 4 in wheelbase
Price: £1,600

1940 Chrysler (USA)

phaetons

These two striking cars were built by Chrysler as publicity vehicles, some say to counteract the stigma of the unlovely Airflows of 1934 to 1937. Unlike the Airflows, however, the Newport (below) and Thunderbolt (right) were not made for sale, only six of each being built. However, they were seen by a vast number of people as they were taken across the country for exhibition at shows and the more important dealers' showrooms from the winter of 1940 through the summer of 1941. The Newport dual-cowl phaeton was the Pace Car at the 1941 Indianapolis 500-Mile Race. Both had bodies designed and built by LeBaron, the Thunderbolt being the more advanced, with its retractable metal top and straight-through lines that would not seem old-fashioned today. It was named after Captain George Eyston's Land Speed Record car of 1937.

Engine: 8-cyl, 82.5×124 mm, 5,300 cc. Coil ignition, side valves, 143 bhp
Transmission: 3-speed, shaft drive, 95 mph
Chassis: channel-steel frame, four-wheel brakes. 10 ft 7½ in (Thunderbolt), 12 ft 1½ in (Newport) wheelbase

1946 Cisitalia (I)
coupé

Cisitalia (Consorzio Industriale Sportivo Italia) was a textile, hotel and banking conglomerate headed by Piero Dusio, who decided to build small Fiat-based racing cars immediately after the Second World War. His success with these led him to try a two-seater, also Fiat 1100-powered, designed by Giovanni Savonuzzi, and the first of these was ready by mid-1946. The car illustrated is the second two-seater chassis, fitted with a coupe body designed by Alfredo Vignale, who was later to become one of Italy's best-known coachbuilders. Although not a beautiful car by present-day standards (Pininfarina later made a much better-looking coupé for Cisitalia), it had a number of advanced styling features including the fins and portholes, both of which were later taken up by American stylists.

Engine: 4-cyl, 68×75 mm, 1,089 cc. Coil ignition, overhead valves, 60 bhp
Transmission: 4-speed, shaft drive, 105 mph
Chassis: tubular-steel frame, four-wheel brakes, 7 ft 10 $\frac{1}{2}$ in wheelbase

1946 Krueger Special (USA)
sports car

This car originated in 1934 as a home-built machine constructed by Theodore Koslov with a body of his own design and construction and a model 'A' Duesenberg engine. After the war it was acquired by Mr Krueger, who replaced the Duesenberg unit with a Marmon V-16 tuned to give 225 bhp. Krueger intended to build replicas of this car to sell for $15,000 each, though where he hoped to obtain a supply of Marmon V-16 engines is not known. No cars were built for sale, which is unfortunate as they would have had an electrifying performance as well as very attractive lines.

Engine: 16-cyl, 79.3×101.5 mm, 8,046 cc. Coil ignition, overhead valves, 225 bhp
Transmission: 3-speed, shaft drive, 115 mph
Chassis: channel-steel frame, four-wheel brakes. 8 ft 2 in wheelbase
Price: $15,000

1947 Alfa Romeo (I)
coupé

The first Alfa Romeo of the post-war era was the 2500, very similar to the pre-war models although with updated bodywork. Two models were available, the Sports with 90 bhp engine and 9 ft 10 in wheelbase, and the Super Sports with a three-carburettor 105 bhp engine and 8 ft 10 in wheelbase. There were also three competition coupés built on the short wheelbase, with 145 bhp engines. These had a short but successful competition career, winning the 1949 Circuit of Pescara and finishing second in the Targa Florio and third in the Mille Miglia, all in 1949. The car illustrated is a 'Villa d'Este' coupé on the Super Sports chassis. About 1,500 Alfa 2500s were made between 1947 and 1952, when they were replaced by the mass-produced 4-cylinder 1900.

Engine: 6-cyl, 72×100 mm, 2,443 cc. Coil ignition, overhead valves, 105 bhp
Transmission: 4-speed, shaft drive, 102 mph
Chassis: channel-steel frame, four-wheel brakes. 8 ft 10 in wheelbase

1948 Talbot-Lago (F)
coupé

The Talbot-Lago was one of the small band of French luxury car makers who struggled on after the Second World War in the face of crippling taxation which imposed a tax of nearly £100 a year on any car of more than 3 litres' capacity. The cars had big 6-cylinder pushrod overhead valve engines which were used successfully in Grand Prix racing cars as well as in road-going machinery such as the coupé illustrated, which is of 4½-litre capacity. This has Belgian coachwork, and is seen in company with the contemporary Standard Vanguard saloon. The standard factory coachwork on Talbot-Lagos at this time was much more staid, with saloons and drophead coupés of pre-war appearance. The big Lagos were made up to the early 1950s, being supplemented by a smaller 2.7-litre 4-cylinder car of similar appearance, and the last cars of all had other makes of engine, including BMW, Maserati and Ford.

Engine: 6-cyl, 93×110 mm, 4,482 cc. Coil ignition, overhead valves, 170 bhp
Transmission: 4-speed, shaft drive, 110 mph
Chassis: channel-steel frame, four-wheel brakes. 10 ft 3 in wheelbase

1948 Tasco (USA)
coupé

Shortly after the Second World War a group of American sports car enthusiasts proposed to build a new car under the name Tasco (the American Sports Car Company). The designer was Gordon Buehrig whose best-known previous work was the Cord 810. For the Tasco he used a standard Mercury V-8 engine, a shortened Mercury chassis and a two-seater coupé body somewhat reminiscent of the cockpit of a light aircraft. This was built for Tasco by the well-known coachbuilders Derham of Rosemont, Pennsylvania. An unusual feature of the design were the fibreglass spats on the front wheels, which turned with them. Although the Tasco performed well, its sponsors could not raise sufficient capital to put it into production and only the one prototype was ever built.

Engine: 8-cyl, 81×95 mm, 3,917 cc. Coil ignition, side valves, 95 bhp
Transmission: 3-speed, shaft drive, 100 mph
Chassis: channel-steel frame, four-wheel brakes

◄1948 Veritas (D)
coupé

The Veritas was the best-known of a number of small makes which emerged in Germany shortly after the Second World War, using the pre-war BMW engine as a base. This unit, suitably tuned, was mounted in a tubular frame, and a variety of bodies were fitted, including single-seater racing cars as well as sports cars and road-going coupés and convertibles. The designer Ernst Loof included twin-wishbone independent front suspension and a de Dion rear axle in his specification. In 1950 Veritas introduced a new engine with single overhead camshaft in place of the BMW's push-rods, which was built for them by the Heinkel Aircraft Company. This unit powered sports and racing cars which were given the name of Meteor. The car illustrated is a Meteor coupé. Veritas production was strictly limited, and only forty cars were made in five years of manufacture.

Engine: 6-cyl, 75×75 mm, 1,988 cc. Coil ignition, overhead valves, 100 bhp
Transmission: 4-speed, shaft drive, 110 mph
Chassis: tubular-steel frame, four-wheel brakes. 7 ft 2 in wheelbase
Price: 22,000 DM

1951 Chrysler (USA)
coupé

The first of a series of post-war Chrysler dream cars, the K-310 was styled by Virgil Exner of Chrysler and the body built by Carrozzeria Ghia of Turin, Italy. The prototype cost only $20,000 for all development and building, and Chrysler considered putting the car into production. However, it would have required a separate factory, which was not considered feasible in America, while European plants did not have the capacity.

A rather similar design was built by Ghia to the order of the French Chrysler dealer, and four hundred of these were sold in 1952–3. A convertible version of the K-310 was built in 1952, but like its predecessor only one was made.

Engine: 8-cyl, 82.5×124 mm, 5,300 cc. Coil ignition, side valves, 180 bhp
Transmission: 3-speed, shaft drive, 110 mph
Chassis: channel-steel frame, four-wheel brakes. 10 ft 5½ in wheelbase
Price: $20,000 (prototype)

1952 Cunningham (USA)
Coupé

The cars built by Briggs Cunningham at West Palm Beach, Florida in the 1950s had no connection at all with the earlier American cars of the same name (see page 41). Cunningham was a millionaire sportsman who entered car manufacture with the express purpose of gaining an American victory at Le Mans, and although he never succeeded in this aim, he built some very impressive sports cars during the attempt. The Le Mans cars were stark two seaters, mostly open, although there was a coupé version as well, and these were raced only by the Cunningham team.

The cars sold to the public were more luxurious, with Italian-made bodies by Vignale, and Chrysler V-8 engines. Only two styles were offered, the coupé illustrated, and a convertible. In 1955 Cunningham closed down his racing department as it was proving too expensive, and the Vignale-bodied road cars disappeared at the same time.

Engine: 8-cyl, 96.83×92.07 mm, 5,420 cc. Coil ignition, overhead valves, 180 bhp
Transmission: 4-speed, shaft drive, 145 mph
Chassis: tubular-steel frame, four-wheel brakes. 9 ft 2 in wheelbase
Price: $15,000

1952 Daimler (GB)
limousine

The DE36 straight-8 Daimler was the largest British car of the early post-war era, and was popular with royalty, not only in its home country. The British Royal Family had four, and others were used for the royal tours of Australia and South Africa; DE36s were also supplied to Prince Rainier of Monaco, Queen Wilhelmina of the Netherlands, Emperor Haile Selassie of Ethiopia and the President of Czechoslovakia. The car illustrated has a more flamboyant body than most of its kind, this being by the French coachbuilder Saoutchik. It was ordered by King Ibn Saud of Saudi Arabia for his son Prince Talal. The overall length was nearly 22 feet, and the weight $3\frac{1}{4}$ tons.

Engine: 8-cyl, 85×120 mm, 5,460 cc. Coil ignition, overhead valves, 150 bhp
Transmission: 4-speed, shaft drive, 83 mph
Chassis: channel-steel frame, four-wheel brakes, 12 ft 3 in wheelbase
Price: £3,860 (standard limousine)

1953 Fiat (I)
coupé

Introduced in 1952, the Fiat 8V caused a considerable sensation for it was the first all-new sports car to come from the giant Italian company since before the war. Designed by Dante Giacosa, it had a 2-litre V-8 engine, integral construction and all-independent suspension. The engine was intended for a prestige saloon, but this was never built, and only 114 8Vs were made during a two-year period. The coupés were successful in a number of second-rank Italian races and hill-climbs, but never really made their mark as sports cars. The photograph shows a second-series model whose headlamp arrangement foreshadowed that of the 1962 Triumph Vitesse. Some competition models had five-speed gearboxes, but these were not standardized on production cars.

Engine: 8-cyl, 72×61.3 mm, 1,996 cc. Coil ignition, overhead valves, 114 bhp
Transmission: 4-speed, shaft drive, 119 mph
Chassis: integral tubular-steel frame, four-wheel brakes. 7 ft 10½ in wheelbase
Price: 2,850,000 lire

1954 Lancia (I)
coupé

The Lancia Aurelia saloon was launched in 1950, the first new design of the post-war era from this famous Italian company. It had a 1,754 cc V-6 engine and four-speed gearbox mounted on the rear axle. A year later it was joined by the B.20 coupé, which had an engine of nearly 2 litres' capacity (2.4 litres for 1954). This handsome car is regarded as one of the great post-war classics, for as well as being an excellent vehicle for long-distance touring, it had a distinguished racing record for several years. Successes included 2nd place in the 1951 Mille Miglia behind a specialized sports/racing Ferrari, victory in the 2-litre class at Le Mans the same year, and 1st, 2nd and 3rd in the 1952 Targa Florio. Later modifications to the B.20 included a larger engine of 2.5 litres in 1953 and a de Dion rear axle in 1954. It remained in production until 1959.

Engine: 6-cyl, 78×83.5 mm, 2,394 cc. Coil ignition, overhead valves, 118 bhp
Transmission: 4-speed, shaft drive, 112 mph
Chassis: integral-construction frame, four-wheel brakes. 8 ft 8¾ in wheelbase
Price: £3,472

1955 Mercedes-Benz (D)
coupé

The Mercedes-Benz 300SL had its ancestry in the aluminium-bodied coupés which heralded the German company's return to motor sport in 1952, finishing 1–2 at Le Mans, and 1–2–3–4 at the Nürburgring. Eighteen months later, in February 1954, the 300SL was announced; in effect a road-going version of the W194 racing coupés, though the engine was in fact more powerful. It was an in-line six with fuel injection, canted at an angle of 18 degrees to give a lower bonnet line. The feature that the 300SL is best remembered for were the gull-wing doors which extended into the roof.

These were necessitated by the high sills which, in turn, were an inevitable part of the tubular-frame structure. There was also a roadster, but it was less attractive than the coupé, and fewer were made. Production of the gull-wing coupé lasted from 1954 to 1962, during which time about 1,400 were made.

Engine: 6-cyl, 85×88 mm, 2,996 cc. Coil ignition, overhead valves, 240 bhp
Transmission: 4-speed, shaft drive, 140 mph
Chassis: multi-tube chrome molybdenum frame, four-wheel brakes. 7 ft 10 in wheelbase
Price: £4,393

1955 Pegaso (E)

sports car

The Pegaso was one of the most exciting designs to emerge in the early 1950s, and was the first high-performance Spanish car to be made since before the Civil War of 1936—9. It was designed by Wilfredo Ricart, who had been responsible for the pre-war Ricart-España, and embodied a V-8 engine with two camshafts per bank of cylinders. The five-speed gearbox was mounted on the rear axle. The original Pegaso of 1951 had a 2.5-litre engine, but this was gradually enlarged to 2.8, 3.2 and finally 4.7 litres. The latter was the Z.103 series, of which the two-seater sports car is illustrated. Unlike the earlier cars, this had a pushrod overhead-valve engine in place of the four camshafts, but even so developed 300 bhp. The Pegaso was not an unqualified success; like all sophisticated machinery it required expert maintenance, and its brakes never matched its performance. Total production between 1951 and 1957 reached about 125 cars, of which only four were the Z.103 model.

Engine: 8-cyl, 95×82.5 mm, 4,681 cc. Coil ignition, overhead valves, 300 bhp

Transmission: 5-speed, shaft drive, 135 mph
Chassis: platform frame, four-wheel brakes. 7 ft 8 in wheelbase
Price: 600,000 ptas ($15,000)

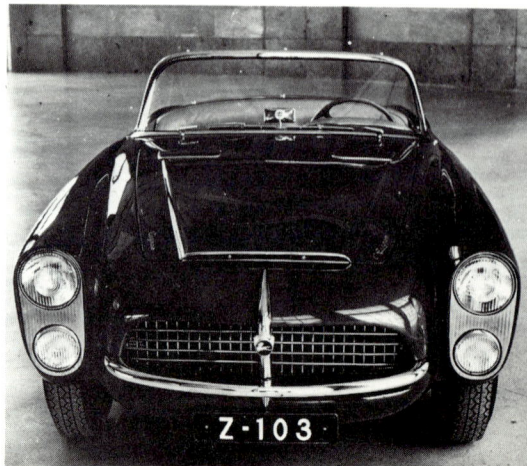

1956 Bentley (GB)
Continental coupé

The first post-war Bentleys were extremely well-built and comfortable cars that shared many features with the contemporary Rolls-Royce Silver Wraiths, but they were of undeniably staid appearance, and hardly lived up to the company's pre-war slogan, 'The Silent Sports Car'. All this was changed, however, with the appearance in 1952 of the Continental coupé. On the standard chassis, stylist J. P. Blatchley designed a beautifully aerodynamic fast-back coupé body which was built largely of aluminium alloy by the coachbuilders H. J. Mulliner & Co. Ltd. The Continental coupé weighed 460 lb less than the standard Mark VI saloon, and had a maximum speed 15 mph faster. Production of these R-type Continentals ran from 1952 to 1955, although the prototype was tested in 1951, and 208 were made. The great majority had Mulliner bodies as illustrated, although there were a few with less handsome Abbott bodies. The Continental name was continued on the S-type made from 1955 to 1959, but the later cars were heavier in appearance, and lacked the superb grace of the R-type.

Engine: 6-cyl, 92×114.3 mm, 4,566 cc. Coil ignition, overhead valves, 160 bhp
Transmission: 4-speed, shaft drive, 119 mph
Chassis: channel-steel frame, four-wheel brakes. 10 ft 0 in wheelbase
Price: £4,890

1956 Kurtis-Chrysler (USA)
convertible and sedan

Frank Kurtis was America's best-known builder of midget and Indianapolis-type racing cars in the 1940s and early '50s, and among his other products were four-wheel-drive aircraft-handling tractors. In 1955 the Chrysler Corporation received an order from a Saudi Arabian prince for two cars with four-wheel drive suitable for desert use. The cars were otherwise standard Chrysler products, but the FWD conversion was entrusted to Kurtis, who is seen at the wheel of the convertible in the photograph. This was used for tiger-hunting expeditions, while the sedan was a harem car. They were in use for at least ten years, possibly longer.

Engine: 8-cyl, 96.83×92.07 mm, 5,426 cc. Coil ignition, overhead valves, 250 bhp
Transmission: 3-speed automatic, four-wheel drive, 105 mph
Chassis: channel-steel frame, four-wheel brakes. 10 ft 6 in wheelbase

1957 Gaylord (USA)
Convertible

The Gaylord was the result of the brothers Jim and Ed Gaylord's ambition to build 'the ultimate car, the sort that would make a man sell his wife into slavery if necessary to buy one'. It had a massive tubular frame, Chrysler V-8 engine, and body designed by Brooks Stevens and built by Spohn of Ravensburg, Germany. Among its features were an electrically operated hardtop that could be handcranked in an emergency, and a spare wheel which came out on ball-bearing rails at the press of a button. Only one car was built with the Chrysler engine and Spohn body, the other three

having Cadillac engines and bodies made by Luftschiffbau Zeppelin. The price was originally fixed at $10,000, but reached $17,500 before any cars were sold. After trouble with the bodybuilders, the Gaylords withdrew from car making, having made only four cars. The one illustrated is a Cadillac-engined model.

Engine: 8-cyl, 101.6×98.4 mm, 6,391 cc. Coil ignition, overhead valves, 300 bhp
Transmission: 3-speed, shaft drive, 130 mph
Chassis: tubular-steel frame, four-wheel brakes. 8 ft 4 in wheelbase
Price: $17,500

1960 Jensen (GB)

coupé

After making a few cars with Meadows straight-8 engines, Jensen Motors Ltd turned to the 3.9-litre 6-cylinder Austin engine. This powered the Interceptor saloon and cabriolet, and in 1953 a more modern Gran Turismo coupé called the 541 was announced. This had a fibreglass body, the first example of a four-seater production car using this material, and a three-carburettor version of the Austin Princess engine. The 541 remained in production until 1962, when it was replaced by the Chrysler-engined C-V8. Improvements during its lifetime included disc brakes (1956), Laycock overdrive (1957), and increased body space together with a revised grille (1960). The standard model was a four-seater coupé, but one or two convertibles were also made.

Engine: 6-cyl, 87×111 mm, 3,993 cc. Coil ignition, overhead valves, 125 bhp
Transmission: 4-speed, shaft drive, 112 mph
Chassis: tubular-steel frame, four-wheel brakes, 8 ft 9 in wheelbase
Price: £2,866

1961 Facel Vega (F)
saloon

The Facel Vega was one of the first of the post-war Euro-American hybrids, using American power units in European bodies and chassis. The original model of 1954 was a two-door coupé with Chrysler V-8 engine, at first of 4.5 litres, then progressively enlarged to 4.7, 5.4, 5.8, and finally 6.3 litres. Most Facels were two-door coupés, but in 1960 the company entered the four-door saloon market with the Excellence, an FVS coupé with an extra 19 inches of wheelbase. A total of 230 were made from 1960 to 1964. There was a scheme in the USA to revive the Packard name using the Excellence body and chassis with a Packard V-8 engine and radiator grille, but it came to nothing.

Engine: 8-cyl, 100×92 mm, 5,801 cc. Coil ignition, overhead valves, 325 bhp
Transmission: 4-speed, shaft drive, 120 mph
Chassis: tubular-steel frame, four-wheel brakes. 10 ft 3¾ in wheelbase
Price: £6,376

1963 BMW (D)
saloon

The first post-war BMW was the Type 501 of 1952, powered by a 6-cylinder 1,971 cc engine similar to that which had been used in the pre-war cars. It had a new five-seater saloon body, and this was later fitted with the first of BMW's V-8 engines, a 2,580 cc unit. Thus equipped, the saloon was known as the 502, and subsequent coupé and open-sports models were the 503 and 507. There was also a little-known limousine, the 505, of which only prototypes were made. In 1959 the V-8 was enlarged to 3,168 cc and used in the saloon, coupé and sports models. The car illustrated, known as the Super, is one of the last of this generation of saloon to be made, for the following year they were replaced by the completely new 4-cylinder 1500 series.

Engine: 8-cyl, 82×75 mm, 3,168 cc. Coil ignition, overhead valves, 160 bhp
Transmission: 4-speed, shaft drive, 115 mph
Chassis: tubular-steel frame, four-wheel brakes. 9 ft 3½ in wheelbase
Price: £2,791

964 Aston Martin (GB)
onvertible

ston Martin pursued a steady line of develop-
ent during the 1950s and 1960s, beginning with
he 2.5-litre 107 bhp DB2 and culminating with
he 4-litre 282 bhp DB6 of 1966. All these cars
ad 6-cylinder twin-overhead camshaft engines
eriving from a design of W. O. Bentley. The
ypical body style was a two-door coupé, two
eaters only up to 1954 and then supplemented by
our seaters, although rear-seat accommodation
vas never very spacious. A number of open cars
vere also made, of which the DB5 illustrated is
n example. Production was at the old Aston
Martin works at Feltham, Middlesex until 1958
vhen it was transferred to the former Tickford
ody works at Newport Pagnell, Buckingham-
hire.

ngine: 6-cyl, 96×92 mm, 3,995 cc. Coil
jnition, overhead valves, 255 bhp
ransmission: 4-speed (5 speeds optional),
haft drive, 145 mph
hassis: platform frame, four-wheel brakes.
ft 2 in wheelbase
rice: £4,490

1965 Ferrari (I)
coupé

This is a late example of the Ferrari Superfast, the largest-engined road car the company has produced and, for its day, the most expensive. The line of big V-12 Ferraris began in 1951 with the Tipo 342 America which had a 4.1-litre 200 bhp engine. As its name implies, it was aimed at the transatlantic market, but did not achieve immediate success. The 4.5-litre Tipo 375 of 1953 did better because of greater power, and this was in turn succeeded by a 4.9-litre model in 1955. The Superfast was a development of this, the chief improvement being the adoption of disc brakes in 1959. Superfasts remained in very small-scale production until 1966, a variety of bodies being fitted including the Pininfarina coupé illustrated and others by Boano, Bertone, Ghia, Vignale and Superleggera Touring. In 1965 the Superfast was listed by the Guinness Book of Records as the most expensive production car in the world, with a price of £11,519.

Engine: 12-cyl, 88×68 mm, 4,961 cc. Coil ignition, overhead valves, 400 bhp
Transmission: 4-speed, shaft drive, 160 mph
Chassis: integral tubular-steel frame, four-wheel brakes. 8 ft 6½ in wheelbase
Price: £11,519

1966 Lamborghini Miura (I)
coupé

One of the greatest success stories of the post-war era is that of Ferruccio Lamborghini, who began by making tractors and progressed to central-heating equipment and air-conditioners, before turning to motor cars in 1963. His first car had a front-mounted V-12 engine of his own design, but in 1965 he launched a most striking coupé, the Miura, named after a Spanish breed of fighting bull. This had a 4-litre V-12 engine mounted transversely behind the driver and passenger, but ahead of the rear axle, power being taken by spur gears to a 5-speed gearbox and thence by further spur gears to the rear axle. The futuristic-looking and extremely expensive Miura was intended as little more than a design exercise, but orders were received in much larger numbers than Lamborghini had anticipated and it remained a production model until 1973 when it was superseded by the even more advanced Countach. The Miura was bought by pop stars and Arab princes as well as by sporting drivers.

Engine: 12-cyl, 82×62 mm, 3,929 cc. Coil ignition, overhead valves, 350 bhp

Transmission: 5-speed, spur-gear drive, 180 mph
Chassis: integral-steel frame, four-wheel brakes. 8 ft 7 in wheelbase
Price: 8,160,000 lire

1966 Nissan (JAP)
limousine

The largest Japanese car made in the 1960s was the Nissan President, with a 4-litre V-8 engine and six-seater saloon bodywork. One considerably larger car was made for the Japanese Emperor; known as the Prince Royal, it used the President engine with an extended wheelbase allowing for limousine bodywork seating eight.

Engine: 8-cyl, 92×75 mm, 3,998 cc. Coil ignition, overhead valves, 180 bhp
Transmission: automatic, shaft drive, 95 mph
Chassis: integral-construction frame, four-wheel brakes
Price: not for general sale

1968 De Tomaso (I)
GT coupé

Argentine-born Alejandro de Tomaso built a number of racing cars and experimental sports cars from 1959 onwards, but the first machine that went into serious production was the Mangusta, a mid-engined coupé in the school of a Lamborghini Miura, but using an American Ford V-8 engine, tuned by Carroll Shelby to give 305 bhp. The two-seater coupé bodies were made by Ghia, a coachbuilding company which de Tomaso had acquired in 1967. The Mangusta was not raced and there were criticisms of its handling characteristics. Its successor, the Pantera, was more successful in this direction and competition versions of this have been built. De Tomaso is now wholly owned by Ford.

Engine: 8-cyl, 101.6×73 mm, 4,728 cc. Coil ignition, overhead valves, 305 bhp
Transmission: 5-speed, transaxle drive, 160 mph
Chassis: forked backbone frame, four-wheel brakes. 8 ft 3 in wheelbase
Price: 6,250,000 lire

1968 Mohs (USA)

sedan

Dubbed by its designer Bruce Baldwin Mohs the 'Ostentatienne Opera Sedan', this was one of the most unusual and expensive cars to be built in America in recent years. Mohs' main concern was with safety and to this end the car had no side doors, entry being through the rear. Other features included seats that swung laterally on turns and pivoted to horizontal in the event of a head-on collision. The sedan was equipped with a refriger-ator and two-way all-transistor radio with two base stations for home and office. Prices ran from $19,600 to $25,600 according to the type of engine used, but not more than four of these cars were built, all using the smaller engine.

Engine: 8-cyl, 98.4×81.74 mm, 4,976 cc. Coil ignition, overhead valves. 250 bhp
Transmission: automatic, shaft drive. 100 mph
Chassis: integral-steel frame, four-wheel brakes 9 ft 11 in wheelbase
Price: $19,600

1970 Thomassima (I)
coupé

The American enthusiast Tom Meade began re-bodying sports/racing cars for road use in 1961, operating from a small works in Modena, Italy. A Maserati 350 was followed by a series of Ferrari-engined cars which he named Thomassimas. The car illustrated is the Virginia, based on a Ferrari GTO with 5-speed ZF gearbox. The aluminium body is only 40 in high, the same as the Ford GT40.

Although the Virginia was built for his own use, Meade received at least two orders for replicas, which sold at $15,000 each.

Engine: 12-cyl, 68×68 mm, 2,963 cc. Coil ignition, overhead valves, 314 bhp
Transmission: 5-speed, shaft drive, 170 mph
Chassis: multi-tubular-steel frame, four-wheel brakes. 9 ft 2¾ in wheelbase
Price: $15,000

1971 Stutz (USA)
coupé

The makers of this striking 6.6-litre coupé borrowed the name of the famous Indianapolis-built sports cars of the pre-war era, but the design was entirely up to date, employing a Pontiac V-8 engine, a modified Pontiac chassis and a hand-built body designed by Virgil Exner and built in Italy by Carrozzeria Padana. Most of the Stutzes made have been coupés, but an alternative and even more expensive design is the four-door saloon based on a Cadillac chassis. The makers planned a special open car for parade and ceremonial use to sell at $75,000, but this was never built.

Engine: 8-cyl, 104.7×95.2 mm, 6,558 cc. Coil ignition, overhead valves, 425 bhp
Transmission: automatic gearbox, shaft drive, 140 mph
Chassis: channel-steel frame, four-wheel brakes. 9 ft 9 in wheelbase
Price: $25,000

1972 Ligier (F)
coupé

Although the bulk of French car production today is concentrated in four major manufacturers, there are a number of smaller concerns, one of which is Automobiles Ligier of Vichy. These are built by Guy Ligier, a former rugby football international and racing driver. The JS2 illustrated was a typical mid-engined coupé powered by a Citroën SM V-6 engine, tuned to give 165 bhp. Later versions of the JS2 have used the 3-litre V-6

Maserati engine and there was also a JS3 sports/racing prototype which raced at Le Mans. The initials JS stand for Jo Schlesser, the racing driver who was killed during the 1968 French Grand Prix and who was a great friend of Guy Ligier.

Engine: 6-cyl, 87×75 mm, 2,670 cc. Coil ignition, overhead valves, 163 bhp
Transmission: 5-speed, shaft drive, 160 mph
Chassis: tubular-steel frame, four-wheel brakes. 7 ft 8 in wheelbase
Price: 74,000 francs

1972 Maserati Bora (I)
coupé

Maserati joined the ranks of the mid-engined sports car builders later than their rivals, Ferrari and Lamborghini, their first essay in this direction being the Bora two-seater coupé of 1972. This had a V-8 engine with four Weber carburettors and an exceptionally strong body/chassis construction. Like the Lamborghini Miura, the Bora has not been raced but is one of the fastest road-going cars today. A smaller Maserati of similar layout is the Merak, powered by a modified Citroën V-6 engine.

Engine: 8-cyl, 94×85 mm, 4,719 cc. Coil ignition, overhead valves, 310 bhp
Transmission: 5-speed, transaxle drive, 174 mph
Chassis: integral-construction frame, four-wheel brakes. 8 ft $6\frac{1}{4}$ in wheelbase
Price: 9,600,000 lire

1973 Citroën (F)
SM coupé

This interesting car resulted from collaboration between the French Citroën and Italian Maserati companies, as it had a 2.7-litre V-6 engine made by Maserati though not used in a car of their own until several years after the SM's introduction in 1970. Other features of this very advanced design were a 5-speed synchromesh gearbox, disc brakes all round, six headlamps and the usual Citroën self-levelling suspension. It was the fastest and most expensive Citroën ever made, and among other competition successes it won the 1971 Moroccan Rally. Fuel injection was standardized in 1973, but there were few other changes made until production ended in 1975. The coupé was the only standard body style offered, but a long-wheelbase four-door convertible was built for ceremonial use by the President of the French Republic.

Engine: 6-cyl, 87×75 mm, 2,670 cc. Coil ignition, overhead valves, 188 bhp
Transmission: 5-speed, front-wheel drive, 142 mph
Chassis: platform frame with lateral box members, four-wheel brakes. 9 ft 8 in wheelbase
Price: £4,420 (in 1973)

1973 Monteverdi (CH)

Saloon

Peter Monteverdi joined the ranks of makers of Euro-American luxury cars in 1967 when he introduced his Chrysler-engined coupé with 2+2 bodywork by the Italian coachbuilder Fissore. He followed the fashion for mid-engined cars in 1970 with the Hai and the following year followed another fashion in adding to his range a four-door saloon in the style of the Maserati Quattroporte or Iso Fidia. Like other Monteverdis, this 375L saloon has a Chrysler V-8 engine. It can be obtained in limousine form with division between driver and passengers, and at the 1974 Geneva Motor Show a special version was exhibited with typewriter, tape recorder and bar in the rear compartment. Total production of Monteverdi cars is less than one hundred per annum and of these not more than twenty are the four-door saloon model.

Engine: 8-cyl, 109.7×95.2 mm, 7,207 cc. Coil ignition, overhead valves, 310 bhp
Transmission: automatic gearbox, shaft drive, 140 mph
Chassis: channel-steel frame, four-wheel brakes. 10 ft 5 in wheelbase
Price: 93,000 Swiss francs

1973 Rolls-Royce (GB)
limousine

In 1959 Rolls-Royce extended their range by adding a long-wheelbase chassis for formal limousine coachwork. Named the Phantom V, this has been made in small numbers ever since, an updated model being given the name Phantom VI in 1968. With an overall length of 19 ft 10 in it was, and is, the longest British car made. The limousine bodies were mainly supplied by Park Ward, H. J. Mulliner and James Young, although there were single examples by Hooper and Chapron, and one or two two-door saloons by James Young. Several Phantom Vs and VIs have been supplied to the British Royal Family, including landaulettes with folding roofs, and a perspex roofed limousine. The car illustrated is a Phantom VI with standard limousine coachwork by H. J. Mulliner—Park Ward, the two firms having merged in 1961.

Engine: 8-cyl, 104×91.4 mm, 6,230 cc. Coil ignition, overhead valves, 220 bhp
Transmission: automatic gearbox, shaft drive 104 mph
Chassis: channel-steel frame, four-wheel brakes 12 ft 1 in wheelbase
Price: £15,570

1974 Panther (GB)
limousine

Panther West Winds Ltd of Weybridge are a small concern specializing in handbuilt cars which may be said to be based on pre-war designs, although they do not set out to be exact replicas. The first and best-known Panther is the J72 two-seater sports car, but at the 1974 London Motor Show the Company launched a more ambitious design, the De Ville Limousine. This is reminiscent of a pre-war Bugatti and is powered by a Jaguar V-12 engine. Among its luxurious fittings are electric windows and air-conditioning, while optional extras include an electric sliding roof, radio/cassette player, television, telephone and cocktail cabinet.

Engine: 12-cyl, 90×70 mm, 5,343 cc. Coil ignition. overhead valves, 266 bhp
Transmission: 4-speed, shaft drive, 130 mph
Chassis: channel-steel frame, four-wheel brakes. 11 ft 10 in wheelbase
Price: £17,500

1976 BMW (D)
3.0 CSL coupé

This was the top of the BMW range in performance, and the culmination of a line of 6-cylinder cars which began in 1969 with the 2500. Two years later the engine was enlarged to 2,985 cc in the 3.0 range, while the CSL had a slightly larger engine still, of 3,153 cc. It was made only in coupé form, and has been widely used for racing when a horizontal aerofoil was often fitted above the boot; this feature was forbidden on the road-going cars.

Engine: 6-cyl, 89.2×84 mm, 3,153 cc. Coil ignition, overhead valves, 206 bhp
Transmission: 4-speed, shaft drive, 137 mph
Chassis: channel-steel frame, four-wheel brakes. 8 ft 7 in wheelbase
Price: 42,260 DM

Index